Building Heroes Academy
646 W 630 S .
Orem, UT 84058
www.buildingheroesacademy.com

ISBN 978-1-950757-00-8
ISBN 978-1-950757-01-5 (ebook)

Cover and Interior Design: Abby West

First printing June 2019 / Printed in the United States of America

How to Get EVERYTHING Done

Homeschool and Clean the House and Stay Sane

This book is for my children, who give me a lot of things to do and inspire me to figure out what is really most important!

CONTENTS

INTRODUCTION . . . 7

PART 1: SUPER MOMS!

Chapter 1: Homeschool and Overwhelm . . . 13

Chapter 2: The Hero's Journey . . . 19

Chapter 3: Journey to the Unknown . . . 29

Chapter 4: Myth of SuperMom . . . 33

PART 2: HOMESCHOOL

Chapter 5: What Is Education? . . . 39

Chapter 6: Create the Environment to Learn and Grow. . . 43

Chapter 7: Surround with Ideas of Greatness . . . 47

Chapter 8: Books, People and Greatness . . . 51

Chapter 9: Free Time and Boredom . . . 57

Chapter 10: Avoid Distractions from Greatness . . . 61

Chapter 11: Training and Leading . . . 67

Chapter 12: Obedience and Requiring . . . 69

Chapter 13: Good Questions and Thinking . . . 71

Chapter 14: The Big Picture of Academics . . . 75

Chapter 15: Individual Skills . . . 79

Chapter 16: Family-Style Schooling . . . 85

Chapter 17: A Pattern for Learning . . . 87

Chapter 18: Lighting the Fire . . . 99

Chapter 19: Am I Doing Enough? . . . 103

Chapter 20: Choosing Curriculum . . . 107

Chapter 21: Fitting Homeschool in Your Day . . . 111

PART 3: CLEAN THE HOUSE

Chapter 22: Your Perfect Home Depends on YOU! ... 115

Chapter 23: Principles and Systems ... 117

Chapter 24: Principles of Order ... 119

Chapter 25: Systems of Order ... 127

Chapter 26: Habits and Self-Discipline ... 131

Chapter 27: Self-Discipline ... 133

Chapter 28: Progress, not Perfection ... 137

PART 4: STAY SANE

Chapter 29: Sanity ... 143

Chapter 30: Control, Motivation, and Stressed-out Mommas ... 145

Chapter 31: Stop Worrying, Start Believing ... 147

Chapter 32: More on Worry ... 151

Chapter 33: Be Controlling ... 155

Chapter 34: Self-Care and Sanity ... 157

Chapter 35: Practice Makes Progress ... 165

Chapter 36: Progress and Purpose ... 169

Chapter 37: The Truth About Getting Everything Done ... 173

Chapter 38: You Are a Super Mom! ... 175

WHERE TO FIND GOOD BOOKS ... 177

BIBLIOGRAPHY ... 179

Introduction

Have you ever heard that joke about college students? College students all want three things:

1. good grades
2. sleep
3. a social life

But it's said a college student can only have two out of the three! Which one do you choose to eliminate? We laugh, because for college students, it seems true!

For homeschool moms I think we could tell a similar joke. We all want three things:

1. to homeschool
2. to have a clean house
3. to stay sane (sleep is included in that!)

It seems as if we really can only have two of the three!

I started getting an inkling that I needed to write a book because so many people would ask me, "How do you do it all?" I always think, "What are you talking about? I don't do it all!" Which is true, I don't do it all. I would normally answer "Oh, I do get a lot of things done, but you'd be surprised at how much I don't do. Just don't come look in my storage room. Or garage." But I realized I have figured out how to get a lot of things done, and most of the time I do regularly homeschool, keep my house clean, and stay sane. As I interacted with more and more homeschool moms I could see that it wasn't just me who had struggled mightily with finding that balance. It's tough! Finding the balance didn't come how I thought it would, though.

And that's why this book exists. I'm here to give you hope. You can have all three. If I, the formerly seriously disorganized and unstructured mom of seven can do this, you can too. It won't be perfect, since life was never meant to be that way, but you can have order and homeschool and still stay sane! I know some of you spend a lot of time cleaning the house and can never seem to get to homeschooling the kids, and then you feel guilt because you believe you're failing your kids; and others of you spend time homeschooling and can never seem to get to cleaning the house, and you feel overwhelmed with all the chaos! Still others of you throw yourselves into doing it all with homeschool and keeping the house running, but you're going nuts because you never have time for you. We can have success with all three and they do go hand in hand. (I have seen that some of those college students have figured out how to have to all three of their wants too!)

Fortunately, over the years I've learned a few things. I still way overestimate my abilities to actually get things done in the time frame I come up with (I tend to think like this: "Write a book in two weeks? Sure! I can do that! No problem, I can still care for my daughter with surgery, keep the house running, do my taxes and oh yeah, homeschool the other ones.") But I have learned a few things of how to balance it all and how to write a book in the middle of all the chaos, even if it does take me three months instead of two weeks.

In this book, I'm sorry to say that I won't actually be solving all your problems and help you be perfect with perfect kids and a perfect home. Sorry, not sorry, because I don't think you should be perfect with perfect kids and a perfect home! I'm not even going to actually help you get everything you think you should be doing done. You will be not be sane if you keep on holding to that thought that you can (must?) do all those things on your list. You know I'm talking to you, my friend, with the list that is so long it can never be done. It's not even necessarily written; much of it is that guilt list you carry around with you in your brain. I'm going to help you become more sane so you can pick and choose the most important ones.

I will be giving you you some new ways of thinking about how you really can balance homeschool, cleaning the house and staying sane. I'll suggest some simpler systems that will put you on the track to creating the life you want. This won't be a quick fix, but it will be a good start! My hope is that you'll have great epiphanies about how you can start making your home life run more smoothly.

If you're like me, you love reading good ideas in a book, but often you don't implement them. If you need help on the implementation end of things, know that I'm here to help! I've been there, done that, and I'm still doing it. I know how hard it is. Not only do I have a ton of awesome tools to help you, I'm really good at encouraging and supporting you on your homeschool journey!

Warning: This information has the potential to change your life! You may never have thought of life this way, or maybe you have and you didn't like it or you liked it but didn't know what to do with it. Once you choose to act on these ideas, your life will become one you've dreamed of living!

One's mind, once stretched by a new idea, never regains its original dimensions.

Oliver Wendell Holmes

It's simple. Not easy, but simple. It's a hard path, but it's so purposeful and fulfilling. It's where you want to go, and it's where I want to help take you.

Ready to get started? Let's go!

PART 1
SUPER MOMS!

CHAPTER 1

Homeschool and Overwhelm

It was the day after Christmas, and the house was an utter disaster. And I mean a disaster. Dirty dishes piled high in the sink, laundry overflowing, no beds were made. As you entered the front room, oh wait. You couldn't actually get into the front room because there was so much stuff in there from our Christmas festivities. I'd been looking forward to Christmas for months! Actually, let's be real. I was looking forward to Christmas being over with so I didn't have to do all the traditions, special food preparation, decorating, gift purchasing, card-sending, picture-taking and all that comes with getting ready for Christmas. Plus I was pregnant so I just wanted to relax!

At last it was over, but the house was a mess. We hadn't done any homeschooling in a good six to eight weeks, which meant that the kids had been busy doing other things, like messing things up. Spreading a million parts to games all over, putting stickers on their beds, coloring on things they shouldn't be, eating food and dropping crumbs and trash on the floor, you know how it is.

In less than a week, the new year would begin, and YES! This was the year I was going to get organized! This upcoming year, my house would be spotless. We would do our three to four hours of homeschool every day, and the kids were going to be so well-behaved and never complain about doing their homework. The baby would always sleep in a timely manner and never get teething pain or colic. I would actually go to bed at a reasonable hour and get up perhaps before the kids did and the house fell apart.

Then the phone rang.

"Hello, this is Mr. Johnson. I have some clients who would like to come and see your home this afternoon."

I nearly dropped the phone. Our house had been on the market for four months, and we'd only had two showings. Now we get another showing on the day after Christmas and my house was a complete disaster? It was cold and snowy and we had to pack everyone up and go somewhere? You're kidding, right?

Nope. It wasn't a joke.

So of course I said "Sure, no problem!" and then we frantically began cleaning for the next four and a half hours. We grabbed the three kids and we left. (The children may or may not have had matching shoes on.)

Those people did not put in an offer.

But hey! The house did get clean(er)!

Sometimes I think God has a funny sense of humor. Other times I know He does.

I knew I had to get my act together, but I really had no idea how to do it or even where to start.

You see, at this point, I'd been homeschooling for about four years. When my oldest son was about 3, I started feeling like I needed to homeschool him.

Truthfully, I thought that was a terrible idea. I thought many negative things about homeschoolers, things like "homeschoolers are strange." "Homeschoolers are unsocialized." "Homeschoolers don't do any school and wear pajamas all day (or maybe denim jumpers) and never comb their hair."

I thought many negative things about myself, like "I'm not organized enough." "I don't know how to teach my kids." "I don't even know where to start." "I don't have time for that!"

So I didn't listen to that idea that I needed to homeschool my oldest son. When he turned five and went to kindergarten, I rationalized that I didn't need to homeschool him, because of course the experts know what they are doing, and anyway I could just volunteer in the classroom and be an awesome mom helper.

He went to school, and I was not an awesome mom helper. I was a paper-cutter-outer and stapler-of-pages, and I didn't hardly interact with my own son at all. But the good news was that as I was in the classroom, I began to see that this really wasn't rocket science. (Although rocket science would've been more comfortable for me. I have a bachelor's degree in mechanical engineering!)

During that entire school year, I still felt unsettled about him being in the school, so at the end of the school year, I decided I would "practice" homeschooling over the summer to see if I could do it in the fall.

Let's just say you can't really "practice" homeschool. Either you're all in, or you're not. I wasn't, and my experiment didn't turn out too well.

Since I still felt like I needed to homeschool, I started learning all I could about it. I read lots of books. I surfed the internet incessantly, and I made plans. Oh the plans I made! Seriously long and detailed plans that no actual human being could ever do. But I didn't know that, and I wanted to make sure we were not going to fail. When fall came, I was still feeling this feeling that I needed to homeschool him. So despite my fears and strange thoughts about homeschoolers, I burned my bridge and I actually didn't send him back to school. It was all me and him now!

We began the highly detailed schedule I had created for us to follow for school from 9 am to 3 pm.

The first few days were great! I'd planned fun things to do and we enjoyed the freedom of not having to go to school.

Then reality set in and I discovered something. 6-year-olds pretty much only want to play and create. They don't want to do a ton of school work. My son didn't want to do what I was telling him to. But he had to, right? Because if he didn't then he wouldn't get educated and I would be totally failing him.

The next few months were filled with power struggles and lots of tears. I was aiming to start school at 9 am, but it was taking hours on end to just get us going. We weren't finishing by 3 pm, the curriculum said we had to finish this much stuff in a day, and by golly we were going to if it took till bedtime! Of course I also had a preschooler to entertain, and I was pregnant, which meant I was way too tired to do any housework or cook. We were in survival mode.

Why was I homeschooling when it was basically misery for all of us?

Well, because that voice inside told me that it was what I needed to do. I was no quitter. But something HAD to change, or we were all going to go crazy. It didn't help that my husband just kept telling me if it was too hard, why didn't I just send our son to school? (Or maybe it did help—it made me determined to make it work!)

As I pondered and prayed over this, I got an answer. I'm not sure I recognized it as an answer at the time, but it was an answer all the same. I had been using our read-aloud time as an incentive to get all our worksheets and other school work done. That was definitely my son's most enjoyable activity in homeschool. But we usually never got to it because we were too busy power-struggling. This thought that came to me said "Why don't you put the read-aloud first?"

I argued with that idea. It wasn't "real" learning because he wasn't learning to read, to write, to do math. After a few weeks I decided to try it. Strangely enough (at least to me at this time), it helped!

A few years later we'd created a bit better routine, but I was still struggling. Since I'd first started homeschooling my oldest son, I'd sent my second to kindergarten, because I still was worried I couldn't homeschool them both at the same time. Sending the second one to school just clarified that I really was supposed to homeschool them all.

Why did I feel like I was supposed to homeschool my kids if we were hating nearly every minute of it and the house was a disaster and I was going CRAZY? Why did I feel like I really needed to teach my kids if I just thought I was messing them up and failing them?

I really didn't know. But I believe that things happen for a reason, and I continued to search for answers and pray for help. Sometimes I think we just want all the answers now so it'll all be perfect. But it doesn't really work like that. It's more like a process of improvement.

15 years later after that crazy Christmas day, we have 7 kids. I've homeschooled them all and I'm still in the process of it because I love it now! The two oldest are out of the house, and both have graduated from a prestigious college—one paid for it with scholarships, and the other got a cosmetology license and worked her way through. (Well, one actually did move back in. But don't worry, he is getting married soon and moving into the house he just bought!)

What I didn't know was that when I began homeschooling, I was embarking on an amazing journey of my own. Homeschooling wasn't really about the kids.I mean they, of course were a part of it. But the education wasn't just for them, it was for me too.

Over the years, I have learned many things that I don't think I could learned as successfully had I given up and not homeschooled. I have learned:

- My kids are amazing human beings. They have goodness in them (even when they don't act that way), and they have greatness in them (which is their amazing potential for doing good).

- My kids aren't any better than yours. Admittedly I love mine more than I love yours, but that's ok, because I imagine you love yours more than you love mine. Yours are amazing human beings too. They have goodness and greatness too. I want my kids around kids whose mothers recognize that.

- I will do anything to help my kids live up to their potential. Yes, even change myself and do things that I find uncomfortable.

- It's more important to have good relationships with my kids than to have power struggles to make them do what I want them to, even if I really think they need to do or learn something. It's more important to love them even when they mess up than to shame them into acting how I want them to.

- If I see the goodness and the greatness in my kids and encourage them to live up to that, they will mostly educate themselves.

- I have to see the goodness and greatness in ME so I can see it in my kids and others.

- I don't have to be perfect at this. I can mess up and it's still going to work out.I can trust that inner guidance voice that leads me to what my family needs. I can be confident in homeschooling because I'm trying to do my best.

- As I keep working to improve myself, I'm leading the way and empowering my kids to do the same.

- Creating an environment of learning is way more important than checking off all the boxes of what we and the experts think they need to learn.

- Most of the teaching methodologies in educational systems are best for simply learning facts. Reading great books, hands-on experiences, play and music are much better ways to learn than worksheets.

- Real education is all about seeking for true principles and then applying them to yourself to become better, to live up to your mission in life to help others.

- It doesn't take a lot of time to guide your kids to learn and grow. It takes a lot of mental effort and willingness to change myself to help my kids learn and grow, though.

It was so confusing and chaotic to try to homeschool my kids in the early years because I really had no idea what education was all about. I knew little bits and pieces and they were all swirling around in my head in a chaotic fashion which came through in how I lived my life!

In the next chapter, I will tell you about a pattern that really changed how I saw my life and the lives of my kids. This pattern really helped me start organizing all that chaos in my brain.

CHAPTER 2

The Hero's Journey

About 15 years ago, I attended a homeschool conference where I heard a speaker talk about the hero's journey. I had perhaps heard brief mention of this pattern, but I hadn't thought much of it. Truthfully, I didn't think much of it in the class either. It did, however increase my awareness of this concept, because as the years went by, I kept hearing about it.

I've learned that whenever I keep hearing about things over and over, it's a pattern, and if I pay attention to patterns, I can learn new things that I need to learn that are important for me and family.

So I began paying attention. What I learned about how this pattern applied to my own life, and of everyone else's lives around me was really powerful. I could truly say it changed my life.

Maybe you've never heard of the hero's journey, or maybe you have and didn't think much of it. Or maybe you have and it has helped you in your life! Whatever your experience is, keep your mind open, because this is the lens through which I'm going to tell you how I get everything done, and how you can too.

In the 1980s an English professor named Joseph Campbell wrote a book called The Power of Myth and afterwards filmed a PBS series. He had studied world mythology extensively and discovered that mythology almost always follows the cycle of a "hero journey." Ancient people used this pattern, and we still find this pattern in most of our modern stories too!

Here's a brief overview of the hero's journey:

Ordinary – The hero is ordinary, unaware that he has great power to make a change.

A Call to Action – The hero has an opportunity to act on something that seems really hard, or at the very least uncomfortable. The call is something that he doesn't necessarily want to do.

Refusal – The hero doesn't feel like he can accomplish the task at hand. He feels fear. He rationalizes why he can't do it, and chooses not to do it.

Mentor – The hero may find someone at this point who has been there before and this mentor is able to give him advice, training, encouragement or other help. Or the mentor may show up after the commitment (the next step).

Commit to Acting – The hero realizes that he needs to listen to this call to action and act. He recognizes that the call to action is more than just about him, and he needs to do it. He leaves his comfort zone and dives into the adventure.

Roadblocks – The road isn't easy. The hero runs into tests, traps, trials and temptations. At any time, he could decide it's too hard and quit – but a hero pushes through.

Allies and Enemies – The hero meets allies, which are others who have similar calls to action who can help him along the way. The hero will also meet enemies who try to stop him on his journey.

Major Challenge – The hero faces his greatest fear or death. The hero wants to give up. But success is just around the corner, and it's so big, he can't give up!

The Reward – The hero completes the mission and has not only changed a part of the world but changed himself.

Once you know this pattern, you'll start to see it everywhere. If you pay attention, you'll see it in stories, books and movies.

One of my favorite hero stories is Bilbo Baggins in *The Hobbit*. He starts out in his nice, comfortable life in his hobbit-hole. One night, he gets a visit from a group of dwarves who are on a quest to reclaim their treasure from a dragon who had stolen it. Gandalf, the wizard, believes they need a hobbit to join the quest as a burglar, and calls Bilbo to action. Bilbo flat out refuses, as he'd much rather stay home and eat soup, where it is comfortable! Gandalf, as mentor, encourages Bilbo. Bilbo feels fear, believes he is too ordinary and thinks he can't do something as crazy as go on a quest! His people play it safe. But then he remembers his mother's side, where some of his relatives did do courageous things. Perhaps he does have a bit of his mother's adventurous side in him. He begins to believe that he can do it, so he commits to action by running out to join the party which had already left.

The rest of the story is full of adventure, challenges and heroic deeds. Along the way, they meet friends who believe in the cause and help them, and enemies who try to stop them. They make it to the final battle, and it seems absolutely hopeless. Yet, they still succeed. The bigger success and what really makes this a great story is that Bilbo is no longer the same. He has found that he does indeed have the courage to act in the face of trial.

It's great to recognize the pattern in stories, movies and even advertising, and know why we feel inspired by hero stories, but it's even more important than that.

Why is the hero journey so significant? It's because the hero journey is really a pattern for our lives.

That's why these stories resonate with us; it's because we wonder if we could be heroic too. We love to see the common ordinary person, the underdog, succeed.

You are a hero on the hero's journey. Your children are too. They have their own calls to action they will need to choose to follow or not. Our whole life is a hero journey, and we go through smaller hero journeys every day, week, month, year and so on.

"Ok, I get that," you say. "It's pretty cool, I guess. I hadn't really thought about myself as a hero. I'm not totally sure I am. Maybe. I like to think of my kids like that. But why do you keep saying this pattern is so powerful?"

The hero's journey is what makes our life more predictable. Patterns are very helpful in life, because they can give you predictability. They can help you see a bigger picture of your life when you just aren't seeing it. Good patterns are ones that are pretty accurate in predicting what will happen next.

The hero's journey changed my life because it could give my own life, and the lives of my kids, predictability. It also changed the way I looked at homeschooling, because if this pattern is a true pattern, then it means that I really don't have any control over what my kids do on their journeys except that I can be a mentor to them. If it's a true pattern, then it means that if I or they step on that hero's journey path, it will be hard, but I can encourage them to keep on going because I know what comes next!

In the grand scheme of things, what is education really for? Most people will say you need an education so you can get a job and be a good citizen. While these are certainly worthwhile goals, it's not what education is all about. Education is really all about developing the greatness within, living up to your potential, developing character, and becoming your best self so you can share your gifts and talents to help others.

That's just what happens on a good hero's journey story. The hero is learning, and gaining an education on his journey. He's not doing it to get a job or to be a good citizen, although those things may play a factor in the journey. He's doing it because deep inside, he knows it's the right thing to do.

Let's take a closer look at you on the hero's journey. Your life was going along fine and it was probably pretty **ordinary**. But then at some point, you had a **call to action** when you first started thinking about homeschooling your kids. For some it was easier than others to decide to homeschool, but for many of us, you felt a lot of **refusals**. If you were like me, you probably thought of plenty of reasons why you couldn't homeschool or didn't want to homeschool. You may have even put it off and not done it for a while because your fears were strong; you had no idea how to homeschool. Perhaps you knew some people who homeschooled and maybe some you weren't impressed with but that one **mentor** friend was doing an amazing job and you wanted that too. Eventually, something in you was stronger than the discomfort you felt, and you decided to do it anyway and **committed to act**. You pulled the kids out of school and began the journey even though you had no idea what to do. You figured out a few things, made some things work, but struggled with other things you had no idea would even be a struggle! The hero's journey path has a lot of **roadblocks**, and the path isn't nearly as straightforward as you'd like it to be. You may be lucky and have some other homeschool friends/**allies** to help you.

This is where homeschool moms can get lost. You get lost in the tests, traps and trials. You may have people/**enemies** who are against your decision to homeschool. The life of a homeschool mom is not easy. You find it's difficult to manage everything; you wonder if you are failing your kids. You have no time to yourself (ever). You are juggling all those plates and sometimes they come crashing down. You find yourself lost in the muck of stuck.

This is where the pattern comes in really handy! You don't have to live in that space of struggle. You can reach out to your friends who are on this journey with you. You can realize that the opposition of other people is not a personal attack; it's just that heroes need opposition to grow and to be confident in their own journey.

When you are struggling and you hit the roadblocks or obstacles, you can choose to believe it is really just a learning opportunity, not something that is there because you are a failure, or to stop you on your journey.

You can get a mentor when you can't see to figure out the lesson, and you want to get unstuck and feel motivated and encouraged again. You can keep moving forward with confidence because you know you're on the right path, and you are learning, growing and becoming better all along the way.

It's the same with your kids! You know they are amazing, but sometimes they will get stuck too. But you can't take their journey for them, and if you want them to learn and develop character, they need to have roadblocks. You can really only believe they are good inside, and act as boundary-keeper and mentor to them, encouraging and facilitating help for them, but you can't take their journey for them, nor can you make them take it. Well, you can try to make them take their journey (which is what most of us try to do when we first have kids), but we just end up creating a lot of power struggles which leads to kids with rebellious hearts or kids who are pleasers.

Mostly we keep trying to move our kids on the journeys that we think are best, rather than guiding them on their journeys simply because we don't know a better way. We want our kids to succeed and be good, but we don't really know how to allow them to take their own journeys.

As you view life from the perspective of a hero's journey, you begin to recognize that you are getting calls to action all the time. If you keep rationalizing, or ignoring those calls, you'll never get connected to your goodness (who you really are), and you'll never attain your greatness (who you can become).

You begin to see that when you do choose to act on those uncomfortable, difficult, but good and worthy things, you are going to learn, grow and become. When you commit to acting, you'll find those allies and mentors and other resources that you need to keep moving forward, because you'll begin to see them. You won't be surprised when you hit the hard times; you know these are just tests to help see how committed you are, and to build your character. When things get the very hardest, you just hold on to the faith that this is just another part of the story, and success is just around the corner.

This is the story of your life, your kids' lives, every human being's life. Knowing that this IS a journey and seeing the pattern gives us hope. Life isn't easy! Struggle isn't there because you're messing up or failing the kids. Struggle is there for you to learn what you need to learn in order to go on to the next step. It's the roadblocks that can become transformational in our lives because without them, we would never seek to become better in that area. It's overcoming the struggle that makes it valuable.

Pay Attention Here! This is GOLD: If you currently have a struggle you don't want to keep having, figure out how to overcome it so you don't need it anymore!

A hero's journey is exciting! It makes life fun! Think of how boring your life would be if you couldn't keep learning and growing. The story would be so boring! In *The Hobbit*, if Bilbo Baggins had stayed home and eaten soup, and we just watched his story, no one would want to watch that show, and certainly no one would be inspired to go out and become better. It is really empowering to see the hero journey pattern in your own life, and the lives of those around you.

You can feel more in control of your own life when you choose to live the hero's journey because it's predictable, but also because you realize the only life you can really control is your own. You really can't control other people's lives. You can help them, but you have to allow them to be on their own journeys. That's especially difficult with the people closest to you, but as you take charge of your own life, you can see how it can work, so you can more easily allow others to do the same.

Now, if you don't consciously choose the story of your life, your life will be determined by those around you, by the media, and by the culture of society. The beauty of the hero journey is that you get to choose if you are on the path of the hero or not. That's what I want my kids to know—that they have personal responsibility for their own lives, and they can create it for good.

Problem is, most of us have no idea that we are allowing others to write our hero stories for us. Children are growing up to be adults who don't know who they really are and don't know that they were meant to do great things. I had no idea that I was allowing others to write my story for me and that I had power to change my story until I came across this pattern.

Now that I know that I am responsible for my life, I can allow and teach my children to be responsible to create their lives too.

Intentionally living a hero journey life is exciting. It's hard, uncomfortable, and sometimes scary. But it's worth it, because it's all about following what you believe is right and becoming who you were meant to become. When we don't hear our calls to action, or rationalize them away and fill our life with distractions, it's an even more uncomfortable and difficult place to be because we know deep inside we aren't living up to our potential. When you feel bored, overwhelmed, unfulfilled or depressed, it's usually just a signal that you aren't listening to your calls to action and acting on them.

All human beings can be heroes on the hero journey; they just need to listen and act. Heroes, however, aren't doing this for glory, honor, accolades, money, prizes, popularity, etc. Most heroes are the quiet heroes overcoming internal battles. These outward rewards may still come to people on the hero's path, but it isn't the main motivation.

So what is a hero really?

When you were first handed that newborn baby and looked into his eyes, you saw more than just a homely newborn. You connected on a deep level, you fell in love, and you knew you wanted to help this child live up to the potential you could see in that child's eyes. I call that process "raising a hero", If only you knew how to support your child's journey!

Most people, when they think of a hero, first think of a superhero. A superhero is someone who isn't real. It's a fictional character with superhuman powers. None of us really want to raise Captain America or Superman, because they just aren't real.

A hero is someone who does what is right when it matters. Those are the kind of heroes you watch or read about in the media, where you see someone ordinary doing an extraordinary act. These stories inspire our souls, because we hope we too would have the courage to act the same way in similar circumstances. They are real-life people on the hero's journey.

The Merriam-Webster dictionary defines a hero as:

1. An illustrious (shining brightly with light) warrior
2. A person admired for achievements and noble qualities
3. One who shows great courage.

In this case, we're mostly going for definition #3. Definition #2 might apply, but it's not the aim. Definition #1 could apply to how we see these courageous heroes in more of a spiritual sense!

This isn't about raising kids to be good and great so others can admire them (or admire their parents!). No, **it's all about raising kids who are ALREADY good, and need to learn to discipline themselves to become great, so they are empowered to live an intentional, purposeful life of service and meaning.**

Of course, I don't want to raise kids that think they can only be a hero if they do something amazing one time. Rather, I really want kids who have such strong character that they continually choose to do what is right every single day. They do those small things every day, so if something big does come up, they are ready to act.

A hero is really someone who has spent the time developing knowledge, skills and character, and chooses to do the right thing by connecting with and helping others when opportunities arise.

Here's a great quote on heroism by author Brandon Mull:

"A hero sacrifices for the greater good. A hero is true to his or her conscience. In short, heroism means doing the right thing regardless of the consequences."

When I look at raising my kids that way, it makes homeschooling so much more exciting! Because I'm raising heroes, I can trust that they are going to learn what they need to learn when they need it. I don't have to worry about satisfying the nay-sayers, or finishing all the standards; rather, I simply need to believe, encourage, create the environment, share ideas of greatness, and lead the way.

You picked up this book on *How to Get Everything Done* and maybe you were hoping for some tips and tricks on how to do that. You'll get some of that too, but what you're really getting is a whole different mindset. This is incredibly important because I can't really help you get everything done, because I already know you have way more on your list (and plenty of shoulds) than you could ever accomplish. The fact of the matter is you don't have to do everything you think you need to do. You're going to learn how to get everything done that is important. The other stuff is just a distraction, but you still keep thinking you need to do it all. You don't have to be SuperMom, but in the next chapter, I'll tell you how you can be a super mom!

CHAPTER 3
Journey to the Unknown

The hero journey is an amazing path to willingly choose to take. It's definitely not the easy path, but it is the fulfilling path.

Most people are so used to having other people tell them what to do, it's like their paths are already made for them. So when things don't keep going as planned, or the path ends, people will struggle to know what to do. We as a society aren't used to making decisions and moving forward when we don't know how or can't see the way.

I think this may also be a big part of the reason that people will have a midlife crisis. They've been following someone else's path for so long, but the day comes when they realize they've never done what they really want to do. It makes them feel stuck and their life is pointless. Since they don't even really know what they want to do, they go buy an expensive car!

It is rare that people will take responsibility for their lives and choose the path they want to go on.

It reminds me of the poem, "The Road Not Taken," by Robert Frost.

> Two roads diverged in a yellow wood,
> And sorry I could not travel both
> And be one traveler, long I stood
> And looked down one as far as I could
> To where it bent in the undergrowth;
>
> Then took the other, as just as fair,
> And having perhaps the better claim,
> Because it was grassy and wanted wear;
> Though as for that the passing there
> Had worn them really about the same,

And both that morning equally lay
In leaves no step had trodden black.
Oh, I kept the first for another day!

Yet knowing how way leads on to way,
I doubted if I should ever come back.

I shall be telling this with a sigh
Somewhere ages and ages hence:
Two roads diverged in a wood, and I—
I took the one less traveled by,
And that has made all the difference.

This poem partly explains why we don't make choices for ourselves: we don't want to choose the wrong path. The author laments that perhaps he took the wrong road, but I think in the end, he chose to believe that the road he took was indeed the correct one, as it was the path that most people do not take and it made all the difference for him.

Many of us just wait until someone comes along and tells us where to go, or we just do what everyone else does.

A hero's journey is almost never the road that everyone else takes. It is difficult, but you know it's right because you heard the call to action. (Robert Frost heard the call to walk on the grass!)

Why don't most people take the path of the hero? Partly because we are used to doing what others tell us, but mostly because we don't believe we can. We listen to the refusals, to those thoughts that tell us we don't know how, we can't do that, we aren't good enough, we don't have time or money or support, and so forth.

As you recognize those refusals and you choose to act despite all the reasons why you can't, that is the first step on the path. As you keep moving, you'll have to keep repeating this process every time you hit a struggle, a wall or an obstacle.

What I've found is that all it takes is first believing that you are good and you are doing good. The next step is believing that you wouldn't have been called to action unless you could find the answers and resources you would need to get through the journey.

Too often we stop ourselves because we think there isn't enough, that we are not enough. Stephen Covey called this the "scarcity mentality."

"Most people are deeply scripted in what I call the Scarcity Mentality. They see life as having only so much, as though there were only one pie out there. And if someone were to get a big piece of the pie, it would mean less for everybody else.

The Scarcity Mentality is the zero-sum paradigm of life. People with a Scarcity Mentality have a very difficult time sharing recognition and credit, power or profit – even with those who help in the production. They also have a very hard time being genuinely happy for the success of other people" (*The 7 Habits of HIghly Effective People*, page 219).

Basically, when you're thinking with a scarcity mentality, you think there is not enough to go around. You feel others must get less in order for you to get yours.

He goes on to define the abundance mentality as follows:

"The Abundance Mentality, on the other hand, flows out of a deep inner sense of personal worth and security. It is the paradigm that there is plenty out there and enough to spare for everybody. It results in sharing of prestige, of recognition, of profits, of decision making. It opens possibilities, options, alternatives, and creativity." (*The 7 Habits of HIghly Effective People*, page 219)

We all like to think we have an abundance mentality, and perhaps at times we do. When it comes to ourselves and moving forward on the hero path, abundance mentality is what keeps you moving.

Why? Because you are moving into the unknown. When you agree to follow a call to action, you have no idea how. You don't know what you're going to encounter along the way. You may know what the end goal is, but chances are you cannot see every single step. So you get frustrated when it's not as fast as you think.

It's like stepping into the fog. You can only go a few steps, but once you have, you can see the next few steps. And so it is with homeschooling. It will only work when you choose to believe by actually taking the next few steps without having to know exactly what to do next or how to do it correctly.

If you believe that you either already have or will find the time and resources you need to move forward, you will. If you believe that you don't know how and you don't have enough time, money or support, you will get stuck.

When you get stuck, ask yourself where you are thinking in a scarcity mentality, and how you could shift to abundance. If you're struggling or stuck, that's where a mentor can be extremely helpful.

A mentor can help you find the answer to questions you didn't even know you were asking. A mentor isn't going to tell you what to do, but rather help you find the answer you already knew but couldn't see.

Following the hero journey is tough, but it's so purposeful that it's rewarding!

CHAPTER 4

Myth of SuperMom

Who has ever felt overwhelmed with trying to get it all done? Raise your hand!

I ask that sometimes in the classes I teach, and every single mom hand gets raised. You are not alone, girl.

Totally get it, been there, done that. Have you ever felt like a giant hamster in an exercise wheel? Running as fast as you can but getting nowhere, never making progress? Have you felt like you have so many things to do to keep the household running, not to mention teaching the kids! You want to get everything done, but you're really just so tired. All.the.time. You don't LIKE this feeling, but you have no idea how to get out, unless you just give up and crash, and you don't really want to do that either. You want to get everything done, but you're just so tired!

I first taught this as a class in my facebook group, and let's just say you're not the only one attracted to this title; it was very popular! After I named it "How to Get Everything Done," some of those sneaky little negative thoughts popped into my head, such as, "Yeah, that's pretty audacious! Who gets everything done? I sure don't so how am I going to teach that to other people?"

I do homeschool, I do have a mostly clean house, and I'm pretty sure I'm mostly sane, but how do I do it? Well, I had to give up a lot of the things that were distractions in my life, and I had to learn how to recognize and act on my calls to actions quickly. Homeschool moms do have a lot on their plate, but really, we try to do way too much. This book is mostly focused on helping you learn how to get most of the important things done in a timely manner and feel good about what you are doing. The alternative is scrambling to do it all poorly, and at the last minute, making you feel like a failure. You don't want that!

Ah, the myth of the supermom. There is that part in all of us, that part that really does want to be supermom. We want everything looking Pinterest-perfect, we want to have perfect children, and we want to look and be perfect. However, as long as you're thinking you need that, you will never get there. That's because there will always be someone or something else more perfect than you and your kids. It's very comparison-based, and even if you aren't conscious that you're doing this, a part of you is still subconsciously doing it! It's really just human nature for women! Unless you're aware that we tend to keep getting sucked into this myth of supermom, it'll still keep creeping back in.

A better way is to aim towards moving forward on your own hero journey and becoming better in your way. This builds your confidence and brings you peace.

You don't have to be perfect to homeschool. You homeschool because you felt the call to do so, not because because you felt highly qualified or perfect at it. As long as you are choosing to keep listening to your calls to action and acting on them so you can learn and grow, you're not going to fail your kids.

You felt that call and once you accepted the call and started homeschooling, you started on that hero journey path. You are learning on the way, and it's OK to mess up; it's OK not to be doing everything perfectly right now, because you know the outcome. You know that you're going to have tests, traps and trials but as you keep pressing forward and learning, you know your kids are good and will turn out great (eventually) as they move forward on their paths too. It's so relieving, really. You don't have to be supermom, but you are a SUPER MOM because you are on that hero's journey.

As you can start picturing yourself and your kids on this path, it changes things. You may have felt ordinary and inadequate but that's fine because that's where you start. You accepted the call; you did it! You may have gotten discouraged, overwhelmed, but that's part of the journey, and you don't have to stay there. You only get there because you don't know what it is that you don't know. That's why it's helpful to have a mentor—someone who has been there, done that to teach you what you can't see.

The beauty of this journey is there are great rewards. Once you start getting in your groove and start figuring things out, it is so rewarding to see the awesome things your kids figure out—especially when you didn't even teach it to them. It's so rewarding to see those moments where everyone is actually getting along. It's rewarding to see your kids take responsibility for their own lives and act that way.

This sounds great, right? But how do you actually do it? How do you go on this hero's journey and how do you keep on going?

You've already stepped on the path, or you're considering it. Please know that if you are thinking of homeschooling and you don't do it, you'll have other calls to action to hear, which may or may not be homeschool-related! Just because you've not followed a call to action in the past, it doesn't mean you failed. It just means that you needed more opportunities to learn what it is you need to learn.

In my interactions with homeschool moms, I've found that most moms are very committed. I've also found that many, way too many, moms are wandering around in the wilderness, struggling with trying to do it all, instead of getting through the confusion and moving forward.

Are you feeling lost in the wilderness? Stuck at a roadblock? Have you felt that way before? This is what it looks like to me:

I hear voices in my head such as these:

> I'm such a mess
> I'm so disorganized
> I'll never get it together
> I'm so overwhelmed
> I'm so discouraged
> I'm failing my kids
> I just can't do it
> My kids are a mess
> My kids are so disorganized
> My kids will never get it together
> My husband doesn't support me

Sound familiar to you?

Yeah. These kinds of thoughts are not the kind of thoughts that keep you moving. These are the kind of thoughts that get you stuck, lost in the wilderness. But there's the good news! If you can recognize what's going on in your head, you can do something about it! It means that you have two choices—you can either stay stuck there, or you can learn something from it.

People also get lost on their journey because they don't have a map, but you do because it comes in the form of the pattern of the hero's journey.

Another reason why people tend to get lost is because they forget to look at the map and aim towards their destination. Maybe you don't really know what your destination is. Luckily, that's easy to solve. You simply decide what you want it to be! Then when you start to get lost or struggle, you remind yourself of the outcome.

Sometimes people get lost on their journey because they don't know they are heroes or they forget who they really are. Have you ever looked yourself in the eye in the mirror and told yourself how much you like yourself? Sounds weird, I know. But most of us don't even like ourselves! Try it! This practice of talking nicely to myself has changed my life.

If you're not used to talking to yourself nicely, this will feel like a lie at first. But it only feels like a lie because of what you've been telling yourself! Keep going until you believe it, because you are good and wonderful and amazing. Some things I say to myself are along these lines:

"I am beautiful."
"I like myself."
"I am grateful for my body."
"I am full of light!"
"I am worthy and good."

If you can like yourself as you are, then you can allow yourself to be imperfect on your journey. You don't have to prove anything, and you can allow others to be too. You are a hero! Don't get confused and try to be supermom or someone else you are not. You are amazing and you are on that journey to become better and better—just don't let yourself get stuck in the middle of it or get off the path altogether.

PART 2
HOMESCHOOL

CHAPTER 5

What Is Education?

By now, I hope you've been starting to practice thinking of yourself and your kids as heroes on a hero's journey. I say practice, because it really does take practice to think about your life differently! But you're a hero, and you can do this.

With homeschool, we come into it believing that if we get the right curriculum, then our children will learn what they need to do and turn out fine. Then we start teaching them, and we think that if we can just make it entertaining enough or make them buckle down and do it, then they'll learn what they need to do and turn out fine.

Seems reasonable. Until you try it. Then you find that it's energy-draining and stressful!

That's why viewing homeschool through the lens of the hero journey makes our lives and our children's lives so much happier! That's because it's not about the curriculum at all. It's all about creating the environment of learning and empowering them to succeed and to fail.

We have taken on the responsibility of educating our children, but it's their own personal journey. You can't make them take it. You may have your own idea of where they should go on their journey, but really as parents, our job is to help our children find the path.

Of course it's a little bit different for your kids because they ARE kids. We can't just say 'away you go on your journey" because clearly that would be totally irresponsible. They do need boundaries and training to keep them safe. As homeschoolers, we are also taking on the responsibility of their education.

Except that we sometimes get that confused. As parents, we may think we are taking on the responsibility of their education, but that's not quite right. Our children are really the ones with the responsibility for their own education. You can't "educate" people by making them learn. You can force them to take information into their heads and learn behavior, but that's really called training, and while it may be effective on dogs and even humans, it's not the best method. It's not a true education.

In the last chapter, I defined a hero as someone who has spent the time developing knowledge, skills and character, and chooses to do the right thing by connecting with and helping others when opportunities arise.

To me, education is so much more than just training our kids and creating robots that act how you want them to. You can't make them choose to spend the time to develop character,and you really can't force them to choose to do the right thing either.

I love this quote:

> *What, then, is true education? It is an awakening of love for truth, a giving of a just sense of duty, an opening of the eyes of the soul to the great purpose of life. It is not so much giving words as thought; not mere maxims so much as living principles. It is not teaching the individual to love the good for one's own sake; it is teaching him to love the good for the sake of the good itself, to be virtuous in action because he is so in heart, and to love and serve God supremely, not from fear but from delight in his perfect character.*
>
> *Character is the aim of true education, and science, history, and literature are but means used to accomplish this desired end. Character is not the result of chance, but of continuous right thinking and right acting.*
>
> *True education seeks to make men and women not only good mathematicians, proficient linguists, profound scientists, or brilliant literary lights, but also honest men with virtue, temperance, and brotherly love. It seeks to make men and women who prize truth, justice, wisdom, benevolence, and self-control as the choicest acquisitions of a successful life.* (David O. McKay, "Why Education" Improvement Era, Sept. 1967.)

(Brief sidenote: I know some people may not believe in God, but even modern psychology says that for people to feel fulfilled, they have to believe in a cause or a power higher than themselves—they can't just live for themselves.)

Can you see more clearly how that is a hero?

If parents choose to homeschool, and kids have a responsibility for their own education, what additional responsibilities do parents have when homeschooling?

- Enabling their own education (their own hero journey)

- Providing a foundation of character training and understanding right and wrong

- Creating an environment in which growth and learning can occur

- Facilitating their children's education (being a mentor on their children's hero journey)

That's pretty much it. You are your children's mentor, and you need to be on the path.

But what does that really mean? What is a mentor? A mentor is a guide on the path; it's someone who is on the path of the hero, but because he is ahead or has completed a particular journey, can turn and help others still on the path.

Mentors do the following:

Act as cheerleaders
Help facilitate growth and learning
Give suggestions for improvement (if the student is ready)
Teach
Listen
Avoid judgment
Allow you to fail
Can see your greatness more than you can
Remind you of your potential
Set a great example
Encourage you
Keep on learning and growing themselves
Look deeper than physical appearances
Ask questions
Show, not tell

Mentors don't:

Make you do things
Shame you (especially when you fail)
Focus on what you "SHOULD" be doing
Save people
Think they have to be perfect
Tell you what to do

The word "mentor" comes from Homer's epic poem, "The Odyssey." Odysseus is the king of Ithaca. He leaves to fight in the Trojan War, and while he is gone, he asks his friend, Mentor, to watch over his household and to teach his son Telemachus. Mentor did do his friend a great service, and Telemachus grew up to be a good man. The word Mentor came to mean trusted advisor, friend, wise person. The Greeks used a mentoring system with great philosophers guiding younger students. Today we mostly think of mentoring as business relationships or for troubled kids, but everyone can use a mentor, and be a mentor! Mentoring is a great way to keep yourself on the path, to grow yourself, and to help those around you.

Mentors can come in different forms. Books can be great mentors. But I find that real live people can be the ones that help us the most. There are different types of mentoring relationships that can be free or paid, short or long term, form or informal, groups, etc. Most mentoring relationships are not long-term, and are entered into for specific help, in areas such as finances, education, exercises, etc.

We don't want to fail our kids, and we would like them to at least have some basic knowledge, right? But how are you supposed to guide/mentor your kids through homeschool when you don't even know what to do? You'll get there!

CHAPTER 6
Create the Environment to Learn and Grow

One thing a lot of homeschool parents worry about is gaps. What about "gaps"? By this we mean what if our kids don't know everything they should know? What if our kids get embarrassed if they don't know something?

Who is to say what they SHOULD know? When we feel like there is a structured system of things that kids should know by a certain time, we will struggle more in guiding them on their own paths. Now, certainly there are good things to know. But why must a person know something just because he is 6 or 11 or 15? What happens after we are 18? Who tells us what to learn then?

Kids who love to learn will learn. They will learn more than you could ever teach them! If they know who they are and that it's their responsibility to learn, they will learn what they need to learn. Sure there will be gaps, but every person has gaps in their knowledge base. That's actually a good thing because then there is always more to learn! Humans were meant to be always learning and growing.

That's why I say that it's more important to create an environment of growth and learning than it is to find the perfect curriculum. This doesn't mean that you leave the kids all on their own, of course.

In order to grow, children need certain things. They need to feel loved and accepted, but they also need boundaries of proper behavior. Parental responsibilities include training them to be obedient and to develop good character.

For example, if you're growing a garden, you have to have the foundation of good soil, which is like systems and routines for food and shelter in our homes. These are patterns—which help you have predictability in your life, and help you feel safe. A feeling of safety and security as well as having physical needs provided for is the basis of an environment of growth.

Next, the seed has to be planted, which you could compare to adding the kids to the home. Seeds have to be watered regularly in order to sprout, and in our homes that is like when we love and encourage them. If we get angry with them, or shame them, that's kind of like stomping on those precious little seedlings, although kids are more resilient, and we can right our wrongs. We can't get out there and make the plants grow; it takes patience and consistency. We also know that big plants, those with big potentials like tomato plants, are going to grow so much better when we are intentional about where they are planted and we use cages. That's like our kids—they'll grow much better when we're intentional about creating the environment and we have boundaries. With plants, we'll apply fertilizer and it's up to the plant to absorb those minerals with their roots. With our children, we bring good things to them, but it's really up to them to open their minds and hearts and absorb that goodness.

Another part of creating the environment is to understand how children grow and develop.

BABIES AND TODDLERS

Babies, toddlers and little kids need tons of love and care, and start to learn boundaries and how to do things themselves. You don't make a baby walk, right? They see you doing it, and they copy you. When they fall or don't learn right away, you don't get mad or think you're a failure. In this stage they are super curious and will get into anything and everything. The main thing to focus on in this stage is love and security, and teaching them right and wrong and obedience. They want to be near you all the time, which is how it should be so you can keep an eye on them!

CHILDREN

Children, from about ages 4 or 5 to 12 or 13 can do many things on their own and can understand boundaries better now. They are still curious and love to learn. However, it's usually during this stage that they can lose a lot of their natural love of learning as we try to make them learn things before they are ready. Some kids will submit because they want to please you; others will flat-out refuse and/or throw fits. In this stage, continue with consistency and obedience training, because they need to learn good habits in order to learn how to gain skills. The other major focus is to encourage your kids to love learning (and not crush it!). This doesn't mean you have to make everything entertaining. In fact, if everything is entertaining, a true love of learning won't be developed.

In order to love learning, kids have to be thinking about things. Kids play to learn about the world around them, and as they are playing, they are thinking. Learning is interesting when you make new connections, so if kids are learning something new and they can connect it to what they already know, they will love it. You know how cool it is when you have an epiphany? An epiphany is when you suddenly make a new connection, have a new insight or a flash of revelation. Yeah, it's that feeling! They'll also love it if you continually remind them that they have greatness inside, and that they can learn from failures.

Free time is super important during this stage. Kids need to play a lot and they are learning when they do (and you can too if you watch how they play house. They copy you!). By the end of this stage, it's my hope that my kids are choosing to learn in their free time. But that doesn't necessarily mean that a kid gets all excited about completing a workbook, although it could. They choose to write, experiment, listen to stories and create things when they have free time. It means that as the kids get older, they are choosing to read stories more than play, although they do still play.

How can you tell if your child has had their love of learning "crushed"? Some signals I watch for to see if I'm trying to make my kids do too much are: (1) They want me to tell them exactly what they have to do and they do that and only that. (2) When they don't have something to do, all they can think of to do is something passive (entertaining) such as watching a show, playing video games, using "gadgets" designed to entertain, and the like. It's much easier to be entertained than it is to be actively learning. Being entertained is not the same as learning. Even if there is an educational element to a computer game, it's still not a love of learning. Those games are designed to release dopamine so you get a good feeling when you reach a new level, but it's not really the same as the good feeling that comes from thinking and learning.

If you feel like your child doesn't love learning, stop trying to push it or even do anything academically. Let them play and create, within the boundaries you set. You can also read or even play audiobooks, because reading is key to creating a love of learning. The human brain loves a good story, but it doesn't enjoy being told what to do. Good stories create good patterns of thinking. They will learn so much just by listening, and you don't have to nag them to do things.

TEENAGERS

At the beginning of this stage, you're thinking there's probably no way this kid is getting in college, but this is an awesome time of life for learning. This is where they can do most everything physically for themselves, and they can really take off, but they don't necessarily have all the skills and discipline to do this. They still are bouncing back and forth between wanting to play and doing something great.

Learning isn't measured on a constant, linear line, but rather it curves up dramatically when it all clicks for your children that they are amazing, they can choose to great things, and they can choose to learn the things they didn't particularly care for earlier on but now want to know because it may be important for them. This is where parents focus on getting out of the way, and helping them stay on track with and facilitating their goals. It's also helpful to find other mentors and classes with peers to help them move forward. Teenagers choosing to learn happens fairly naturally if kids love learning, but it doesn't always, and so if it doesn't, you just keep on focusing on the consistency of character, encouraging a love of learning and showering them with ideas of greatness and letting them learn on their journey.

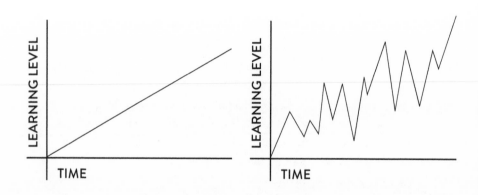

CHAPTER 7
Surround with Ideas of Greatness

If you want motivated kids who know they are on the path of the hero, becoming who they are meant to become, they need to be reminded of that as much as possible! It's so easy to forget, especially when the tests, traps and trials come along.

In addition to using good and encouraging words with them as much as possible to remind them of who they are, you can also surround them with ideas of greatness in your physical environment.

Do people become great because of nature or nurture? That's a big debate that's been going on for thousands of years. Most believe it's both. Humans are born good, and all humans have the potential for achieving their greatness (which is their nature). So why not do all we can to nurture that?

When I first clued into this idea, I had no idea where to even begin. I wasn't great with good words and I spent more time thinking I was a failure. I thought my kids were a mess because they wouldn't cooperate and they would fight and disobey.

I needed to first begin with me. At some level I knew that the hero journey was a true pattern, and if so, I had gotten on it somehow. This meant that I had good desires, and that I followed a call to action which benefited people other than just me. But at a deeper level, I didn't really believe this. So I had to start training myself to believe it! When the negative voices showed up, I'd have to recognize that and choose better thoughts about myself. I had to start to begin to believe in my own goodness and greatness.

At the same time, I needed to start to see the goodness and greatness in those around me and let them know it. As I practiced seeing that in others, I could see it more in myself and more in them.

That's a great place to start!

Another great place to work on too is to make your physical surroundings a place that is always reminding you of goodness and greatness.

What do you have hanging on your walls? I love to hang pictures and sayings that remind us of who we are and what we'd like to become.

What kind of music do you have playing in your home? Or do you even play music? Choose great music that uplifts the feeling in your home. Also consider lyrics to music. We all know that lyrics can get stuck in your head; make sure the lyrics to the music you listen to is putting good thoughts into your head.

What kind of feeling is in your home? How well do the people in your home manage their emotions? If you feel like you have to walk on eggshells because you're never quite sure when someone will explode (or if people feel that way around you), this can be changed! You can have a feeling of peace and love in your home.

What kind of of media is allowed in your home? Is the media encouraging the people in your home to develop good character and reach for their greatness? Or is it distracting them and just filling up time? What kinds of messages are movies, TV shows, books, video games and such sending to your brains about greatness?

How orderly is your home? Is your home generally clean or do you struggle with that? Do you have way too much stuff? Do you have too little stuff? (That's generally not a problem for most of us, but it can be if you don't have resources you may need.) Do you have habits, routines and systems in place? Are they flexible enough? Order brings more peace and calmness to your home, and it's a great way to allow the ideas of greatness into your minds, because a confused and chaotic mind doesn't have much room for more. (Don't worry, we'll talk more about how to have a clean house and homeschool in upcoming chapters too.)

To surround your family with ideas of greatness, think of how you can feed your family's brains with good and great ideas and thoughts. I like to picture my home as a smorgasbord of goodness that they can sample from. If I let in too much junky stuff, that's all they are going to choose to partake of. That's because just like with food, there are those things that aren't quite as good for our bodies but we want them because they are easy and appeal to our bodily senses. The things that are good for our minds and bodies are often not quite as appealing at first, but they nourish our bodies and souls.

I know, I wish I had a perfect home that had Pinterest-worthy decor, beautiful music playing all the time, with a feeling of love at home, rare interactions with media and always clean. Then there is reality; it's not that perfect. What it can be, however, is that I can choose to improve all of those things, and thus I have an environment of progress and improvement, rather than one of perfection. I have a friend that says progress, not perfection! This is a great way of looking at life; we don't need perfection right now in most things in our life.

CHAPTER 8
Books, People and Greatness

BOOKS

Books are a key element to surrounding your family with ideas of greatness! If chosen well, they will help you have a greater vision of what you can become, and encourage a love of learning. Good books and great books (also known as "classics") will teach us patterns and truths about human nature, which helps us achieve our potential as well.

A classic is a book or other creative work that makes you think and learn. Really good classics are ones that you can learn new things from each time you revisit them. Some people think that classics must be old to be classic. They don't; many of the world's classics that are old are still around for a reason, which is that the author understood human nature and patterns. That said, any new book that meets those same criteria can also be considered a classic. When I first heard about the power of reading classic books, my main experience was with reading difficult books in my AP English class. I felt a bit intimidated, but I just decided to read children's and young adult classics first, and then I found that reading "adult" classics wasn't so difficult after all but very enjoyable!

Let me give you an example of some words of truth from a children's book, *The Phantom Tollbooth*. Not only is this book very witty so children and adults alike enjoy it, but this book is a great example of a hero journey. It begins with a very ordinary, bored little boy who finds himself choosing to save the two princesses in order to restore "Rhyme and Reason" to the kingdom, and along the way he is transformed himself into someone who can choose to become better.

At one point, he and his friends are traveling along a treacherous mountain path, said to be full of demons. They come across an elegant man with a blank expression who asks them for some help. He is so pleasant that they willingly agree to help him. This man, with no facial features, then asks them to do some very monotonous tasks, such as moving a large pile of sand from one spot to another using only a tweezer.

As they begin their tasks, they feel like they could go right on this same way forever. It's not until they actually become aware of what they are doing and how long it would take to finish that they question the man about the usefulness of their tasks.

"Of course it's not important," he snarled angrily. "I wouldn't have asked you to do it if I thought it was important." And now as he turned to face them, he didn't seem quite so pleasant.

"Then why bother?" asked Tock, whose alarm suddenly began to ring.

"Because, my young friends," he muttered sourly, "what could be more important than doing unimportant things? If you stop to do enough of them, you'll never get to where you're going." He punctuated his last remark with a villainous laugh.

"Then you must---" gasped Milo.

"Quite correct!" he shrieked triumphantly. "I am the Terrible Trivium, demon of petty tasks and worthless jobs, ogre of wasted effort, and monster of habit."

"But why do only unimportant things?" asked Milo, who suddenly remembered how much time he spent each day doing them.

"Think of all the trouble it saves," the man explained, and his face looked as if he'd be grinning an evil grin--if he could grin at all. "If you only do the easy and useless jobs, you'll never have to worry about the important ones which are so difficult. You just won't have the time. For there's always something to do to keep you from what you really should be doing…"

That certainly made me reflect on where I was getting tricked in my life by the Terrible Trivium! What a spot-on truth taught in a great story!

I don't think I've ever met a kid that doesn't love a good story. Some kids do need to be trained to listen, but you can do that by starting out with shorter reading sessions and stopping before they get bored. I always like to have my kids say, "Mom, please read more!" Sometimes I will, but often I won't because I want to leave them wanting more. I also allow any quiet activity such as Lego bricks, coloring, puzzles, etc., as long as they aren't talking (or reading) while I read aloud. Snacks are great because it keeps their mouths full. If a kid doesn't want to sit still for a read-aloud, don't make him! You'd be surprised at how much kids can hear even when it doesn't seem like it.

Way too many kids don't think they like books, but they usually like read-alouds. Often this is because they lost their love of learning when the skill of reading was difficult.

I have one son who I didn't think enjoyed reading because he never would pick up a book, but one day I was surprised to learn that in his mind, he thought he loved reading. This was because we had made it a point to always be reading in our house with daily read-alouds and listening to audiobooks. He loved stories, but reading was a bit difficult for him. But because he loved stories, he did finally get to the point where he started picking up books on his own around age 12-13.

The human brain loves stories. In fact, it's a good thing because our brains can learn lessons through stories much more readily than we can if someone just tells us. It's a much more powerful experience to hear the story of "The Tortoise and the Hare" than to tell a kid not to be lazy, to just keep going and to be persistent. It's much more enjoyable to read great stories to my kids than to nag them!

In the book, *Once Upon A Brain: Homeschool Edition*, the author Thomas Morley teaches through story about how your brain learns best through story. One character, Jill, says, "So, what is wrong with pointing out correct ways to think and behave?"

Her friend, Mary, answers, "Nothing, except it rarely works, even when your arguments are logical and defensible." She then quotes a study where,

> *"...researchers found that our brains don't like to be contradicted. The researchers hooked subjects up to an fMRI brain scan and provided them with solid evidence that either supported or contradicted a deeply held misconception. When the information matched well with what a person already believed, the information was processed in the portion of the brain that deals with learning and long-term storage (memory.) No surprise here. When the information contradicts one of their fundamental beliefs (the misconception), neurons fired that had more to do with error detection and conflict resolution than with learning. Anomalies or contradictions automatically shut down the avenues of learning because they trigger the wrong types of neurons."*

Jill is surprised by this and replies, "You're kidding me. So you're saying much of the nagging I've done through the years has literally fallen on deaf ears?"

Mary responds with, "It gets worse. In a related study, researchers found that simply telling a person over and over that they are wrong still didn't change their views. The subjects continued to shut down their learning neurons and activate their error detection brain cells."

Basically, telling people what to do or where they are wrong doesn't work. But as parents we still want to teach our children. Our children's brains are open to stories!

However, if a story is obviously moralizing, or if we have to put our two cents worth in "You see, in this story you should learn…," it still has the same effect of shutting down our learning.

We have a lot of books in our home, because there is just something about having books that makes you feel like reading. But you don't want to pick just any books. Choose the best books you can.

How do you know what good books are? Here a few guidelines:

1. Find lists of "good books." There is a list at the end of this book of lists of good books. Start out by choosing from those lists.

2. Good books encourage greatness. Choose books that are uplifting, with good values and proper respect for the human body.

3. Ask trusted friends or mentors for book recommendations.

4. What books changed your life? Revisit those books.

5. Choose stories that have a hero cycle in them.

If you think you can't afford a lot of books, it doesn't have to be costly. You don't have to own thousands. Shop at thrift stores, used bookstores online, or library book sales (find out when the last day is for big discounts). But do have some books you own, because your belongings show your kids what you value, and physical books remind you to read. You can also go regularly to the library, as well, of course. There are also digital books, which can be great, but the one problem with digital books is that you can't see them on a bookcase, and they become "out of sight, out of mind."

PEOPLE

People are another great resource to surround our families with greatness.

As motivational speaker Jim Rohn says, "You are the average of the five people you spend the most time with." That's because the people you spend the most time with shape who you are. They affect your thoughts and how you feel. They add to your ideas of goodness and greatness, or take away.

I'm sure you know some people who just make you feel good! You know others that are energy-suckers and you don't want to spend a lot of time around them. Be intentional about who you choose to be around and learn from.

How do you find people who encourage you? You look for them! If you're looking, you'll find them.

But what if your current friends bring you down? Find new ones. What if it's your family? Then you get to be the chainbreaker. A great place to find people who will remind you of your greatness is to take courses and hire a mentor.

I love homeschool co-ops for the fact that I can choose who is hanging around my kids. If you don't have one, start one, and invite great people you know to join you. If you don't know any great people, invite people with the intention that great people will come. They will! But not everyone needs a homeschool co-op, so don't stress if you don't want to be in one.

Positive shared experiences are a great way to connect with other people. Anything you do with other people is a shared experience. Choose good experiences with good feelings to share with good people, and it will remind you of your greatness, and do the same for your children. This is one reason I love to homeschool my kids and do read-alouds; it's usually a positive shared experience. If we're in a power struggle, or if we're just generally grumpy, that's a negative shared experience, but it can be turned into positive one when people choose to apologize and forgive and reset the feeling in the home to one of peace and love.

CHAPTER 9

Free Time and Boredom

Part of creating an environment of learning and growth is giving the kids enough time and freedom to explore and play. This free time is so important because that's when they learn and think and grow.

It's easy to overschedule our kids and ourselves so we don't have any time to think and create and refresh. I have to be very conscientious about scheduling in free time in our schedule and holding to that.

During free time, we have boundaries about what they can and can't do. Because I'm trying to be intentional about creating a home that surrounds us with ideas of greatness, that extends into free time as well. It's not that I'm trying to be controlling, but rather that I'm trying to keep them safe and give them good things to choose from.

I like to picture it like this. Let's say you live in a house on a corner lot near two very busy roads. You would want a fence around that side yard to protect your kids from running out into the street before they knew what was good for them. But inside that fence, there are plenty of things for them to explore like trees, a treehouse, toys, chalk, and so on and they can play with any of those things inside the fence to enjoy nature.

It's the same thing inside of our homes. I like to put up a fence of boundaries, and then provide things they can explore there to learn to think and become who they are meant to be.

During free time, they can play or read. If they would like to make something crafty, then they'd need to ask permission first and have supervision, if they are younger and aren't likely to keep things clean. Because the purpose of free time is to play, and the purpose of play is to discover how the world works and to begin to develop thinking processes, I like to encourage creativity! For that reason, the kids aren't allowed on any media during free play time.

It's also why we get toys that encourage creative free play, not toys that entertain.

We want them thinking! Toys that have been favorites at our house include:

- dolls, big and little
- play kitchens with play food
- cash register
- blocks and trains
- pattern blocks
- Lego bricks & other building toys such as K'Nex
- science toys such as slinkies, yo-yos, etc
- dress-ups
- cars
- Playdough
- animals and figurines
- puppet theater
- active toys (roller skates, scooters, pogo sticks, bikes, etc.)
- marble run
- creative supplies such as paper, glue, scissors, arts & crafts supplies, boxes, magnets, pulleys, ropes or yarn, electrical parts, etc.
- board and card games

Of course you don't have to have tons of toys for the kids. They get creative with what they have. If all they have is rocks and sticks, they'll create something!

What about playing with friends? Well, it depends on the friends! What are the friends mostly playing with? Is it creative? Are the friends mostly uplifting or do the kids fight all the time? Are the friends manipulative? If the kid's friends aren't good influences, limit contact! Obviously I'm not saying to make sure these friends are perfect; they're kids! But it's not just about friends. Ask those questions about your own kids. If they are the cause, then limit friends until they can be friends.

Another good thing to look at is how your kids act when they can't play with friends, or if they've been playing with friends all day. I noticed some of my kids getting really grumpy and not wanting to play with their siblings or even be kind to them!

I had no idea what to do about that, but after pondering on this issue, one day I had this thought to simply give my kids a friend budget. I said, "You can play up to three times a week, and up to two hours each time during the school year, and more in the summer." They had to figure out how much time to spend playing. If they used up all their time for the week by Wednesday, they were done! The power struggle was gone and gone, better behavior was restored. Amazingly they still could figure out things to do without playing with friends.

But what if they can't figure out anything to do? What if they say "Mom, I'm bored!"

When your kids are bored, don't feel like you have to be their cruise director and give them something exciting to do. If a child feels boredom, that's the precursor to creativity. They get to think of something to keep themselves entertained if we don't step in! I've read a lot of of articles encouraging parents to let their children be bored because it's not something as a society we particularly enjoy.

It seems that sometimes as parents it bugs us to allow our children to be bored. One reason is because we don't want to hear the whining! To solve that, we just need a system before the complaint comes up. Decide ahead of time how to act when they say, "Mom, I'm bored!" and then calmly stick with what was decided. For example, if my kids say they are bored, I say, "Oh good! I have lots of things to keep you busy. Would you like to wash the dishes or sweep the floor?" I don't hear "Mom, I'm bored" very often.

Another reason we might not want our kids to be bored is perhaps there are certain activities we don't want them to be doing when they are bored. Solution: Set up your environment (as much as possible) so that they only can choose from good things.

Another issue: what if they don't do anything? What if they aren't productive? What if they aren't motivated? We have to reframe our thinking on that, and remember they are children. Sometimes when it looks like they aren't doing anything—or even it might look like they are wasting time, they are processing, thinking, creating. It just doesn't look like that to us.

That said, I think we need some cautions on allowing boredom.

1. Boredom can lead to trouble. Make sure you have boundaries in place—clear standards and rules about what can and can't be done.

2. Check up on the kids periodically to see where their creativity is leading them!

3. Allowing boredom doesn't mean to let them do whatever they want all the time. Teach discipline and habits and goals, and as they get older they will learn to choose time in a more productive way. But they also need to use that time to think and ponder.

4. Entertainment screen time shouldn't be an option if you're trying to use boredom to spark creativity, because otherwise, that will ALWAYS be the go-to. It's a numbing activity, not a creative one.

5. When a child chooses something creative to do, don't shut them down because it's messy. You can teach them to clean it up!

Allow your kids to be bored!

CHAPTER 10

Avoid Distractions from Greatness

You've probably noticed a theme in this book so far. The one where I keep talking about greatness? That's because it's such an important concept! It's what keeps you on the hero journey!

I know it can seem much more tidy, concrete and clear to homeschool by teaching knowledge the experts say our kids need and by checking off all the boxes that tell you when they are "done." It seems like it can be very effective. But without building character, without knowing who you are and without knowing you can become better, it has very little meaning other than maybe to get a job, and even that is no guarantee.

That's why there needs to be the foundation of knowing that you and your children (and all human beings) are good. Because you are good, you learn discipline and character. Then because you have discipline and character and you know you are good, you want to help others. You do that by becoming better, and journeying on the path to true greatness.

Problem is, that journey isn't easy. There are SO many distractions along the way. We may step on the path, committed to action, but then when the test and traps come in, we get distracted! (Think of the "Terrible Trivium" from the Phantom Tollbooth.)

That's why I took a whole chapter earlier to talk about how we can surround our homes with ideas of greatness. But we also need to avoid the distractions from greatness as well. We forget so easily!

What is distracting you and your family from pursuing greatness?

A big one is media. By media, I mean all screens, including video games, tv, videos, apps, phones, computers, etc. I also include books and audiobooks in this as well. I'm not anti-media, but I am certainly one who wants to evaluate media and how it affects me and my family. Media can be a wonderful tool. It's what is helping me write this book! But there is a big difference between using media as a tool and as entertainment, and either can be overused.

A big problem with screen time is that most of our interaction with the screen is passive; it requires little to no thinking. And even educational screen time is dangerous; they are gamified so your brain chemicals are artificially manipulated to feel good, and the brain becomes trained to be entertained all the time. It kills creativity, and creates humans who need to be entertained all the time or else they are bored and don't know what to do with themselves.

Media is an interesting dilemma because in 6,000 years of recorded history, we have never had media like we do today. We didn't even have mass media until a hundred years ago, when moving pictures became popular. Today we all have it easily accessible in our pockets! The dilemma is how to best manage media—do we allow unlimited access, restrict it completely or find a happy medium? There isn't a precedent or a pattern to follow for managing media. There are, however, patterns to follow for successful living.

Here are some questions I ask about media to figure out how to manage it:

1. What is the message of this media? Is it distracting us from moving forward on our path? Does it encourage us to move forward on our paths? Does it make us want to be better people?

2. Am I using this media as a tool or as entertainment? Does it cause me to avoid connecting with my family? I mostly use media as a tool to get things done; however I discovered that in my quest to get things done, I was not building relationships with some members of my family and I had to adjust! Others use media solely as entertainment, and can have the same problem occur.

3. Are we using this media as an avoidance or numbing tool? I get that sometimes you just need some down time! But too many of us are successfully using media to avoid doing things, or to numb our emotions that come up when we can't handle life too well anymore. Am I using this media to avoid anything? Am I using this to numb feelings or a situation that I should face? Or do I simply choose to use this media as entertainment right now to decompress?

4. Are we on media too much? Am I addicted to it? Do I check Facebook throughout the day when I really don't need to?

5. How does media affect our moods? Are kids grumpy when asked to get

off screens? Are they grumpy after they play a game or watch a show? Throughout the day, does anyone get too easily frustrated, have meltdowns over little things, or become too hyper? Some kids can get overstimulated nervous systems after too much screen time, and they can't manage themselves properly!

6. Are screens usually the go-to when there is free time? If kids can't think of anything else to do when they have free time, or if it's the first thing they always think of, that's a problem. They want to be entertained and to be told what to think, rather than think of something creative to do.

Sometimes the only way to really know how media is making a difference in your life, to know whether it is distracting you or encouraging you, is to go off it. Take a media fast and see what the differences are; it's really eye-opening! Try one week, but if some kids are still complaining about it, keep going until they forget, so you can see how life really could be.

There is some very interesting research in the book, *Reset Your Child's Brain* by Victoria Dunckley, M.D., where she targets "Electronic Screen Syndrome" as the cause of many of our children's struggles today.

> *Screen-time affects our brains and bodies at multiple levels, manifesting in various mental health symptoms related to mood, anxiety, cognition and behavior. Electronic Screen Syndrome (ESS) is essentially a disorder of dysregulation. Because it's so stimulating, interactive screen-time shifts the nervous system into fight-or-flight mode, which leads to dysregulation and disorganization of various biological systems. Sometime this stress response is immediate and obvious, such as while playing a video game. At other times the stress response is more subtle, taking place gradually from repetitive screen interaction, such as frequent texting or social media use. Or it may be delayed, brewing under the surface but managed well enough, then erupting once years of screen-time have accumulated.*

She also suggests a four-week program to help with this, which may be worth checking out if you are seeing any of this in your home.

I know it's not practical to never use media. But be intentional about it and aware of how you use it.

Another distraction from greatness can actually be other people. People can encourage you, or bring you down. If you have friends that bring you down, find new ones that encourage you, and you start encouraging your other friends.

What if it's your family members or relatives that are distracting you for your purpose? In most cases, you're not going to go get new family members! In that case, you just have to be more firm in your commitment to be on this path, and to allow them their journey too.

One more people distraction: Experts! Experts can be wonderful, but if they are making you question yourself and your path that you know you should be on, they can distract you. They may also make you feel like you're not "doing it right." Experts are helpful to get new ideas from, but the real expert is your inner guidance system.

For homeschool moms, a big distraction from education can actually be curriculum. That sounds funny, but it's true! Let me explain. This goes along with experts. We start to feel like we have to do everything the curriculum (as the expert) says. We must finish this one-year curriculum this year at all costs, even if we hate it; otherwise we assume we are failures. Hopefully we've established by now that you may fail, but you're not a failure. Curriculum is a fantastic tool—if you stay in the driver's seat, and don't let it drive you. Be willing to change it up—go faster or slower, mix and match, pick and choose. Also ask the same questions you asked about media, about the curriculum!

Lastly, as you know, we are all our own worst enemy. It is our own thoughts and feelings that can really distract us from greatness! If we allow ourselves to listen to those negative voices and feelings of worry, self-doubt and fear, it's going to get us stuck or off the path all together!

Another way we distract ourselves is through busy-ness. Sometimes we're busy because we're too disorganized. Sometimes we're busy because we haven't learned the skills of "getting everything done." Sometimes we're busy because we want to avoid really looking at what we need to change in our lives.

Watch out for those distractions, because those are the most difficult ones to see. If you need help learning how to get through this, to stop listening to those negative voices, find a mentor to help you.

One of my favorite quotes is by Marianne Williamson.

"Our deepest fear is not that we are inadequate. Our deepest fear is that we are powerful beyond measure. It is our light, not our darkness that most frightens us. We ask ourselves, 'Who am I to be brilliant, gorgeous, talented, fabulous?' Actually, who are you not to be? You are a child of God. Your playing small does not serve the world. There is nothing enlightened about shrinking so that other people won't feel insecure around you. We are all meant to shine, as children do. We were born to make manifest the glory of God that is within us. It's not just in some of us; it's in everyone. And as we let our own light shine, we unconsciously give other people permission to do the same. As we are liberated from our own fear, our presence automatically liberates others."

While she's not specifically talking about distractions, we use distractions so that we don't have to light our lights shine. That puts us in a struggle cycle because we are avoiding becoming the person we are meant to become.

It's a good question to ask yourself what is distracting you and your family from what is really good and great. Then get rid of that distraction!

CHAPTER 11

Training and Leading

I used to think, "If only I were perfect at this mothering thing, I could really do a great job at it!" But it wasn't set up like that in this earthly life at all, and we were still allowed to have kids!

That's the beautiful thing I discovered over time. I don't have to be perfect to guide my children's education. I just need to know a little bit more, or at least be willing to learn it with them.

I also thought it was crazy that I went through 16 years of school and still didn't feel any where near qualified to educate a kindergartner! But that's a whole other story.

Interestingly, the word "education" comes from two Latin words: "educare," which means to train or to mold, and "educere," means to lead out. While the two meanings are quite different, they are both represented in the word **"education."**

To be given a true education, children need training in discipline and obedience, and they need examples leading the way.

Before a child can be trained, they need to know who to follow. The word discipline is interesting, because it comes from the Latin word "disciplina" which means instruction or knowledge, which is derived from the Latin word "discipulus" which means learner and would be translated as "disciple." Disciple means "follower or student of" someone.

Thus, in order to be disciplined, one must have someone to follow or learn from. That is the role of parents. Families are set up in a perfect system for discipline where the children have the parents to follow. Children can learn to obey parents as their parents are consistent in disciplining by instructing and teaching and following through, and children learn to be disciples as they learn to govern their wills to obey.

However, generally humans don't follow people they don't think are worth following. (Although that does happen!) If you want your children to be disciplined, be worth following. If you want your child to become the person he is meant to be, lead the way and start becoming the person you were meant to be. If you don't have the self-discipline you need, start developing it instead of blaming, complaining or beating yourself up. If you mess up, that's OK too. Failure and mistakes are how we learn! You can admit you were wrong, apologize, forgive, learn something, whatever it takes to get back on track. In fact, it's good not to be perfect all the time simply so your kids know it's OK to fail too! If you're working so hard to be perfect for your kids, what lessons are your kids learning?

Once your kids know whom to follow, it doesn't always mean they will follow. We all like to make our own choices. As parents we can try to make it easier by teaching them from our own experiences, but there really are those kids who have to try it themselves. Then when they mess up, you're there to lift them up and encourage them, instead of thinking you're a failure because your kid messed up.

CHAPTER 12

Obedience and Requiring

Our children aren't just something to fill with knowledge and train. As parents we want children who are obedient and do good things. We can try to make them do that, and our children may obey and do good things because we tell them to. What happens when they're out of the house?

While it might be really nice to have 100% obedient kids, if you really think about it, you don't really want that. If you did, you'd just get robots because those would be a lot easier. But you wouldn't connect with them or love them like you do your own children. We want kids who choose to obey and choose to do good things, without us making them do this!

Our children aren't something we train like a puppy; our children have wills of their own, as I'm sure any parent has noticed. When a puppy does something "naughty," it really isn't the puppy consciously choosing to do that, it's more a lack of proper training. If we just wanted trained kids, all we need is to really consistently follow through with rewards and punishments in all behaviors we wanted to shape. While I'm all for training kids to obey, we also need to allow our kids to learn or think or choose the good in life.

In my home, I use chores, requests, and skills to train my children to obey and develop good habits. This is so they have a solid foundation of learning to discipline themselves to obey (most of the time, anyway).

When it comes to school work, however, it gets a little stickier. If I require my children to study and learn, they end up doing the minimum just to get it done. This can obviously still happen with chores too, but most of the time that depth doesn't matter as long as it is done. When it comes to learning, however, just doing the bare minimum doesn't foster a love of learning. That's partly why so many kids lose their love of learning during the elementary years; they are required to learn something so they do the bare minimum, and they never get excited about it or learn the joy of learning. When kids get to the point they think long enough about what they are learning to make a connection, that is exciting! But mostly it's easier to just think long enough to get the right answer and move on.

We want our kids to choose to want to learn more, just like we want them to choose to obey and choose to do what is good. As we allow them this choice, it is amazing what they can learn and how fast they can learn it. We can allow this choice by going back to the hero journey and believing that they are good and will choose to learn.

It's important to set boundaries and clear expectations, to be sure. If you want to train on obedience and self-discipline, you have to have clearly defined expectations and consequences that you've planned ahead of time so you can calmly allow your children to choose if they will obey or not.

I'm not going to go into how I train in obedience in this book, because there are a lot of parenting books that explain how to do that. I don't even do it perfectly, but enough so that it works!

CHAPTER 13

Good Questions and Thinking

In the last chapter I talked about allowing your children to make choices. That is scary, because they could make "wrong" choices. We know in the grand scheme of things that this is ok, because that's how they learn, but we also know that if you can avoid bad decisions, you can also avoid the corresponding negative consequences and still learn.

One thing that can help your children make better choices is for you, as their mentor on this path, to develop the skill to ask good questions of your children. When you ask good questions instead of just telling them the answers, they can figure out their own answers and make their own choices that lead to good.

This is definitely a learned skill, because it seems so much easier to tell your kids repeatedly what they should do! It's not easy to let your kids think things through for themselves. If you're asking questions with the "right" answers in your mind and you have an agenda, you're not letting them think; you're doing the thinking for them!

But what if your kids do make a bad choice? What if they choose the easy-out, the chicken-out, the cop-out, the flat-out wrong or rebellious choice? That's where boundaries come in handy.

A friend of mine had a teenage daughter that really wanted to attend a dance. Their home rule was that you couldn't attend a dance until you were 14 years old, and this girl was still 13. Rather than flat-out denying this teenager this choice, her mother asked her good questions such as, "What do you think the right thing to do would be?" and then allowed her daughter to think about it and make her own decision. The daughter decided that it was OK for her to go to the dance. So her mother supported that decision, but then also put in the boundary that she or her father was going to go with her as a chaperone.

Sometimes you can't talk to your kids because their hearts are feeling too rebellious. In that case, write them notes about how good they are! Sometimes you can't even give them the notes, but write them anyway; it changes your heart and how you are treating them.

In *A Jane Austen Education*, by William Deresiewicz, the author hits the *mentoring* nail on the head. He's getting his PhD in English, and he has a professor who at first seems eccentric and silly. He says about the questions he asks, "They seemed absurdly simple—silly, really, almost stupid, too basic and obvious to ask a class of freshmen, let alone a graduate seminar. But when we tried to answer them, we discovered that they were not simple in the least. They were profound, because they were about all the things we had come to take for granted…"

Later, he says, "Within about half an hour, I had started to get what the old man was doing, and I realized that I had never experienced anything like it before. He was stripping the paint off our brains. He was showing us that everything is open to question, especially the things we thought we already knew. He was teaching us to approach the world with curiosity and humility rather than the professional certainty we were all trying so hard to cultivate. In order to answer his questions, we had to forget everything and start over again from the beginning. 'Answers are easy,' he would later say. 'You can go out to the street and any fool will give you answers. The trick is to ask the right questions.'"

It's SO tempting to just tell the kids what they should learn. I still battle this. A much better way is to ask questions and let them figure it out at whatever level they are at. If they can come up with a solution, they will be more likely to follow through and act on that than if you just tell them.

Of course you don't want to just ask questions. A mentor is also a good listener, so learn to draw your kids out and get them talking about themselves in ways they don't usually do. Help them make connections between what you're learning and themselves. Ask questions like, "What does this remind you of?" "How could this apply to someone's life?" and so on.

Before you can mentor a child, you need to have a good relationship with that child. Ask connecting questions like:

> How was your day? (This can elicit a solid good, ok, or bad answer, so just ask follow-up questions.)
> What is your favorite thing to do?
> Tell me about what you did today.
> If you could have any animal in the world, what kind would it be?
> Tell me about the book you're reading.
> What would you like to do this week?

Here are some great questions to ask a child who is struggling with something to help them find a solution:

> Do you have anything that is bothering you?
> You said you are struggling with… Why do you think that is?
> What could you do to change that?
> Is there something I can help you with?
> How do you feel about this?
> What is scary about this situation?
> What could you change about it so it's not so hard/scary?
> What do you know about this already?
> What do you think you need to know about it to solve this problem?

For helping children pursue a goal (that they set, not you), try some of these questions:

> What do you want in your life? What would be really cool to be/have/see/do?
> What goals do you have to get there?
> What type of activity do you need to do to accomplish that?
> Are you willing to do the work?
> Who could help you accomplish this goal?
> What resources do you already have?
> How strong is your commitment (1-10)?
> If it's not a 10, why not?
> What kind of person do you need to become to accomplish that?
> Are you willing to change to become that person?
> How can I support you in this goal?

Don't just sit down with your child and read all these questions. Use your intuition to know what questions would help your child right now. These questions are just to get you thinking!

CHAPTER 14

The Big Picture of Academics

You probably never thought of homeschooling as creating the environment and leading the way, did you? I wanted to start with that part because that's what makes homeschool doable.

You could sit with your kids and try to teach each one individually for eight hours a day. (Or even with just one!) But you're a busy mom with lots to do! So it makes a lot more sense to empower them to learn.

But still, when will they learn academics? Knowledge is important too!

One thing that really helped me was to see the big picture of academics within the educational framework. While it's great to see yourself and your kids on a hero journey, it is really helpful to see what knowledge can be learned too.

One reason we get overwhelmed with homeschooling is because we can't see the big picture—we have some nebulous idea of what needs to happen and we have no idea how it's going to happen because we aren't really sure when we get there. When we went through our years of schooling, we never saw the big picture of what we were being taught.

One problem is that the educational system has taken everything apart and compartmentalized it into dozens of different subjects and made it seem like we have to learn all of these every year or our child will get behind.

That's why it's helpful to see the big picture.

We can divide knowledge into four main subjects: Math, Language Arts, Science and Social Studies (aka history/citizenship). Within each main subject, you can divide into subcategories as in this chart. If you don't see the big picture, this is where you can overwhelm yourself with 16 different subjects each day.

HISTORY	SCIENCE	MATH	LANGUAGE ARTS
Ancient Middle ages Renaissance Modern Arts, Music	Biology—life: animals, human, plants Earth & Space Chemistry Physics	Patterns, numbers, order Addition/ Subtraction Multiplication/ Division Time & Measurement Fractions, percents, ratios Problem solving & thinking	Reading Handwriting Writing (creation) Mechanics Poetry & Lit Foreign Language
Story of the world	**Observation to explain the world**	**Language to explain the world**	**Communicate about the world and your world**
Stories	**Observations**	**Patterns**	**Communication**

This is the basic pattern for elementary school. But this pattern repeats in middle school, high school, college, and should hopefully keep on continuing for the rest of our lives!

This body of knowledge is all about the world. History tells us the story of the world and about human behavior (if we learn stories, and don't just focus on memorizing dates). Science and Math both teach us how to explain our natural world, and how we relate to it. Science is focused on observing your world, and Math brings a language to explain it with patterns. Language Arts is about developing the skills to communicate these stories, observations and patterns we are learning.

All of these subject areas are about finding patterns. Remember what I said about patterns? Patterns are wonderful because they make our life more predictable! When you know the patterns, you feel more safety and security, but you also know how to move forward as well.

Memorizing knowledge for knowledge's sake isn't helpful because it has no meaning. It's not until we figure out how knowledge connects to our own lives that it has meaning. You've all had that experience of memorizing information for a test, and then forgetting it all as soon as you were done with the test, right? But when we can apply knowledge to ourselves to make our world and the world of those around us better, that's when it become powerful.

If all learning is based on the stories in history insofar as possible, it becomes fascinating. History is full of patterns and stories (and if you remember, I mentioned earlier that stories are how our brains learn best). Turns out that our brains love finding patterns, and it's integral to learning! Research has shown that certain parts of your brain activate when you find a pattern.

Back to history. All those subjects can be learned by basing everything on history, even math! It helps you see how all knowledge is connected.

Many homeschoolers end up doing history-based studies, because knowledge all relates to history, and comes back to relating knowledge and skills to yourself. So for K-6, it's simple to teach your kids the story of the world and how people tried to explain the world with math and science, and teach them skills so they can learn more about the world and apply these concepts to themselves so they can become the people they were meant to be.

How do kids gain knowledge? What teaching methods do you use?

Reading
Telling Stories
Teaching Facts
Seeing: observing and imagining
Listening: stories and songs
Doing: hands-on activities and experiments
Exploring
Being in nature
Discussing
Playing
Presenting (students teaching or telling others what they know)

There are other methods that can be used, and are the ones that are most often used in the traditional school system. These are actually the least effective way to remember new knowledge, because they are mostly based in passive, rather than active, learning. Active learning requires thinking, and creates new neural pathways in your brain.

Here are examples of passive thinking teaching methods:

Lectures

Worksheets

Videos

Our brains remember things from two methods: repetition or emotions. Repetition is a traditional method of learning, because it is effective and efficient—no need to focus on individuals, if you repeat it enough eventually most kids will get it. These methods and repetition are great for practicing skills and learning facts.

If we want our kids to learn to think, we need active learning models. If we focus on creating enjoyable learning experiences for our children, learning becomes much more simple and our brains will retain the information more easily. Plus if they feel good about learning, they will learn so much more quickly.

Typically when you're learning through repetition, it's disconnected information. When you learn through play and having fun, you are connecting it to a greater web in your brain and it sticks better. You are making connections to things you already know! This method that attaches good emotions to learning is great for learning knowledge and how to think.

I'm not talking about entertaining experiences. If you have to do a song and dance and make it fun every time, you're going to get exhausted! Plus it turns into passive learning because there is no thinking involved by the person being entertained.

For my kids, I want them to have a lot of knowledge. But I don't really want to have to give them all that knowledge. I would much rather have them self-educate insofar as possible; however, at these younger ages, they have no idea what is out there.

Instead of giving hours a day of systematic instruction, I aim for enlightening experiences. I simply hold school with them for about an hour a day and introduce them to interesting knowledge. During this time, we do all those things. We read books, tell stories, learn interesting facts, do hands-on activities, go on nature days, etc. I tell them interesting things and we discuss it. We share cool ideas!

CHAPTER 15

Individual Skills

Knowledge is defined as facts, information, and skills acquired by a person through experience or education.

Skill is worth talking about separately. Skill is defined as the ability to do something well. A skill is something that takes a lot of practice to develop. Often, in a public school setting, you don't have enough time to practice something to gain that skill. If you don't learn that skill as fast as the rest of your class does, you get left behind. That's one huge advantage for homeschool families; you have the time to practice skills.

But it's also a huge disadvantage for homeschool families, because most of us are so busy trying to do it all, we don't get around to practicing skills consistently, and often we avoid it because we don't want the power struggle that comes when we tell our child what to do. Of course this could also be a huge advantage for homeschool families, if we train for character and teach how to be consistent in developing new habits.

What are individual skills that our children should learn? .

These are the skills I like to focus on during the elementary years, or by the time the child is 12 to 14 years old This doesn't mean the child will be PERFECT at them; sometimes it's just "good enough" and they'll continue developing many of these skills as a teenager.

CHARACTER	ACADEMIC
Obedience	Reading
Household skills	Handwriting
Good daily habits (get dressed, brush teeth, etc)	Writing
How to set a goal	Typing
How to complete a project	Grammar/punctuation/spelling
How to create a good habit	Math facts (addition/subtraction)
Social skills	Math calculations
Music practice	Computer used as a tool (word processing, etc.)
Spiritual practices (praying, etc)	Memorization
Planning/time management	
Consistency/routines	
Playing an instrument	

This doesn't mean I start off teaching all these skills at age 5. We pick a skill and work on it, when they are ready.

As you can see, there aren't really that many academic skills to develop. It really is readin', ritin' and 'rithmetic! If you have the luxury of waiting until they are ready to learn these skills, it doesn't take long. You don't have to be practicing all these skills all the time. You don't even have to review that often, because likely they are using these skills in their further learning. If your kids have most of these skills by the time they are 12 to 14 years old, they can be successful self-directed learners as teenagers. If they don't, they can certainly still get these skills and still be successful. I had most of the academic skills as a teenager and college student, but when I got married I realized I didn't have most of the character skills. I could still learn them; it just took me a lot longer!

Children grow and develop at different rates. We all know that. Yet somehow we still get fearful when our children seem to be behind the benchmark of what some expert says they should have learned. If a child wants to learn something or is at least willing, they will learn it so much faster than if we keep trying to make them learn.

I've now taught seven kids how to read. They all read at a completely different pace! My first son went from beginning phonics at the beginning of first grade to reading the Harry Potter books in six months. He was ready. My next daughter started learning when she was a little bit younger. But it took her years (about four years, actually) of consistent practice to get to the level of a Harry Potter book. It didn't mean she was dumb or behind; it just meant that she had her own way of learning to read. My next three children (all 2 -2.5 years apart) all learned to read at about the same time. Yep, they were about 4, 7 and 9 years old. My sixth child wasn't going to read as long as I thought it was a good idea, so I had to back way off until he decided to read at age 7.5. He went from basic phonics to a 4th grade level in two months. Now with my last child, she's more like my second child in reading pace.

I tell you this because it's not just with reading. It's with all learning. I had my own little experiment where I could see this with seven kids in retrospect. But most of you can't see this up front—that all these kids are going to learn at their own pace.

I love this garden analogy: Do all seeds grow into the same plant? Do they all grow at the same speed? Of course not! It's just like that with your kids.

How do you know when they are ready for individual academic skills? Here are a few guidelines:

- They can understand the material and learn much of it on their own. (Obviously there are some things you'll have to help with, such as reading.)

- They are willing to try. Willingness is huge in avoiding those power struggles that you don't need. (You help them get to willingness by believing in them!)

- They have the desire. Desire can go a long way when practicing a skill that is hard. It can keep you going!

- They ask for it. Some will, and others never will.

- They are open to the idea when you offer it. This is for the ones that don't ask for it! I offer my children the opportunity to learn skills. But I don't require it. If they don't choose it, I still love them. I've had to disassociate myself and my wants for them to allow them to choose. I will often offer a reward for consistent practice just to get them over that initial difficult hump, or when they get stuck. But I make it clear that it's for the practice of the skill, not for learning.

- They are a bit older. Most of the academic skills I don't even offer until they are 9 or 10, and even then, many of these skills I just wait to see if they figure it out naturally! If they haven't learned to spell well by the time they are 12, then we'll do a unit on that. But a lot of my kids have just been natural spellers and haven't needed it. For the younger kids, I may offer reading, handwriting and maybe math facts. Then again, some of the kids have been able to get those skills when they are younger, so it really just depends on the kid.

What happens if they're working on a skill and they don't want to put in the work? Well, it depends on the kid! If a child "hits a wall" and is frustrated and you're having power struggles, often it just means it's time to take a break. Just stop, and come back later. However, there are some times when the child just needs to push through and keep going. Sometimes they just need encouragement to keep on going and not give up, and they often will without an extra power struggle. Use your intuition to know which method is needed. Praise all successes!

Let me give you an example: My youngest daughter really had the desire to learn to read, but sometimes it is really hard to practice this skill. She can get really frustrated and want to give up, but usually if I just give her a good pep talk, she'll do it. "Oh you got this! You're going to be such a great reader once you get this. I know it's hard, but I know you can do it."

But there have been other times when I knew her brain was just not quite getting it. So I knew it was time to take a break. I just say, "How about we take a break from reading lessons for a few weeks? We can play games (or do nothing) instead."

What are some tools you can use to teach skills? First, remember that you'll learn faster if you are enjoying it. But skills do need practice and repetition. Find that balance!

- music – great for memorizing!

- games – lots of great games for reviewing.

- flashcards & worksheets – but only if the child likes them.

- listening – listen to songs, chants, other audio

- competitions & challenges – do personal best competitions, track your progress, do family challenges. But always have them be optional.

- visual reminders – hang signs on the wall, quotes, etc. What they see goes in their brains. I keep meaning to try this one: Hang a multiplication chart by the toilet! (This is called "bathroom schooling!")

- your example – you practice something. You don't have to practice everything you want them to learn, but practice something.

Have fun! It doesn't have to be boring and repetitious. But you don't also have to do a song and dance to entertain them all the time. Of course if you want to, you can sing and dance and laugh and be silly, but you don't have to. Give them a safe environment to grow at their own pace—allow for lots of stops and starts. Celebrate small successes! Don't expect perfection!

Remember! It's much easier if you have readiness and willingness!

Skills take way longer than we think to become proficient. They aren't adults, they are kids. Even adults struggle at learning new skills. Don't introduce a skill and then expect them to be playing piano at the level of Rachmaninoff within a month. Remember, when teaching skills that they are practicing. Let yourself have that same luxury too.

When my kids are ready and willing, that is the best time for them to learn the individual skills they need.. I don't have to direct hardly at all when we do it this way.

Sounds great, right? But still how do you do it? You've got to teach knowledge and skills and character and you're barely keeping your head above the water in running the house? Let's simplify!

CHAPTER 16

Family-Style Schooling

When I first started out with homeschooling, I was doing one-on-one with my son for about seven hours a day. When my daughter got to school age, I sent her off to kindergarten because I couldn't fathom how I could teach two kids at the same time during the day!

Turns out she ended up having major food allergies, so she needed to come home to be homeschooled. It was inevitable anyway, as it was tricky to have one in school and one not. That's when I learned it was really quite a simple thing to homeschool family-style.

It's a mindset shift from how we learned in public school. In public school, we are trained that everyone must learn the topics of their grade level. But in family-style learning, we can learn any topic all together; we just learn at whatever level we are on. If you think about it, that's how you would learn in school anyway—on whatever level you are on.

Some standards say that children should learn about ancient Greece in the 6th grade. Who is to say that is the best time to learn it? What if a child were to learn about ancient Greece in 1st grade, and again in 5th? The best time to learn about ancient Greece is when you're interested in it, and/or when someone around you is interested in sharing it with you. It's somewhat arbitrary that it is assigned to 6th grade.

Some skills certainly do build upon prior knowledge and skills. In which case, that's where I say let the child learn that when the child is ready. I had one son who could do algebra problems in his head when he was seven, but he couldn't for the life of him remember his addition facts. If we were trying to meet standards, he would be failing, or considered behind. But he did algebra problems in his head because his grandfather taught him how! He had someone interested in sharing with him, and he was interested, so he learned it. And it certainly wasn't a 1st-grade standard.

When I shifted to a family-style, history-based learning format, where we learn everything from a historical perspective, it made all of our lives so much simpler. When I say history-based, I don't mean the way I was taught in school where I had to memorize dates, places and people, but rather with learning the stories of history. Those stories contain all the other subjects in them! I didn't have to teach everything all the time. Initially I switched to this method for sheer efficiency. But something else happened that I did not anticipate.

As we took an hour or two a day to learn together, we built great relationships with one another because we were having a shared learning experience while having fun! We connected with one another, and loved it!

One question I get a lot is from moms wondering how family-style can work when everyone is on different levels. It works *because* everyone is on different levels and will contribute from whatever level you are on. As we teach and discuss with one another, we are all learning! Even mom is learning right along with the kids!

If you think about it, that's how kids are going to learn anyway. Even in a classroom of 30 second-graders, they are all going to learn at their own level, because they are all different.

I've also learned that if I get nothing else done for homeschool but a simple family learning time, it's good; it still works! It's hard to figure out how it will actually work until you actually try it. You can study it, rationalize it, question it all you want, but until you try it, you can't really see how it can work. It's also what makes homeschool doable for families with more than just a couple of kids. (Although certainly you can do family-style learning with just one or two kids as well!)

After family learning time, the kids are still learning. They learn within that environment that has been set up for learning. They also can practice those individual skills that aren't as easy to learn family-style, simply because they are skills that each individual must practice in order to master. Family-style homeschool really works.

CHAPTER 17
A Pattern for Learning

Wait. So to homeschool, do chores in the morning and then plan just an hour a day for family-style schooling? Should they just play all day? Well, maybe!

In this chapter, I want to give you a pattern for learning what homeschool can look like in your home for the various ages of children you may have.

This summer, I was at a family reunion. We went up to Bear Lake, which is a really large, beautiful lake in northern Utah and southern Idaho. Some early-rising family members went to the beach to set things up and save our spot. They popped up canopies and set up our camp chairs and when the rest of us arrived, we all settled in for a fun day in the sun.

As we adults sat around chatting, the babies would sit with their moms or crawl around nearby. The 2 to 6 year olds would mostly dig in the sand and occasionally go dip their toes in the water or grab a bucket of water and bring it back. The 7 to 11 year olds would do all sorts of things—play in the sand, wade out into the water until it got up to their necks, toss frisbees, play on the inflatable rafts or kayaks in the water, but not venturing too far. The teenagers wanted more than that though. They were building massive sandcastles or huge pits and burying each other. They went out on the water trampoline that was 500 yards away, and took out the rafts and kayaks farther than the younger kids would, but sometimes also took younger kids with them.

As adults, we enjoyed ourselves too, occasionally doing some of the fun activities the kids were doing, but we were also keeping a watchful eye out and making sure the kids were all taken care of. We created a spot for their shoes and clothing, sprayed them with sunscreen, prepared lunch, provided life jackets and generally kept things orderly so when the kids came back to the beach, their needs were fulfilled. When one teen ventured too far out into the lake on a raft without a life jacket and we could see she was in trouble out there, her dad asked someone nearby if he could borrow his Jet Ski to go rescue his daughter. Once the other man understood the gravity of the situation, he was more than willing to loan it out, even though the rest of his family was wondering why a stranger was getting on their Jet Ski. Fortunately she was rescued, and brought back to the safety of the beach and her family.

Despite that harrowing incident, some sunburns and seagull droppings, it was a fun, memorable day, and everyone had a great time together.

Later on I was reflecting on this day and I began to think about how much this is like life. So I've come up with an analogy of how this compares to homeschool life. It's a pattern; remember patterns can help you see your life more clearly and and be able to predict what will occur next. As with any analogy it won't be perfect, but then again, neither is life. But I think we can learn from looking at patterns and connections with this, and we'll consider this a pattern for learning and teaching in our homeschools.

Picture you and your husband heading to a beach. You're newly married, so you don't have much; you just plop down some towels and you're good to go. You probably forgot to bring along a few things, or just didn't own some things you may have needed. In life, this is like you setting up your marriage in preparation for children to come, although I'm guessing most of us never thought of it that way! This is where you begin setting up a structure for family life. You probably forgot a few things, didn't know you'd need or want some things. For us on the beach, we wanted a fun experience where the cousins could bond and get to know each other, so we planned for that. In your marriage, you also probably had ideas of what you wanted for your family life, and if not, you did work on figuring that out as you went along.

The beach is also symbolic of the foundation of your life. As the kids came along, you had to adjust. You had to get more resources, such as a shade tent, some camp chairs, a cooler. You had to figure out how to work with your husband to raise these kids. You had to create more boundaries and rules to keep them safe. You teach the kids right and wrong (please don't throw sand in her face!"). The beach, as a foundation, is where the kids will always return when they need something. They come there when they have physical needs. They come there when they get hurt or discouraged or need love. They come there to feel safe. They come there to get things that they aren't going to go to anyone else's patch of sand to get.

Our homes are like the beach, and it starts when we first get married, and then we have babies, the little ones. That's where we are building a foundation and an environment of safety and love. It's also when the little kids are around us the most— which is our biggest opportunity and challenge. (Of course the challenges are where we learn the most!)

With all that in mind, what do you think is most important to create in your environment and with teaching your kids so that they can someday go out and play in the water later on? What skills, resources and knowledge would be important for them to have in these early ages? Now clearly these babies will grow up, but what will make that next stage easier if we teach them, and help them feel more confident? What would you really want them to know before they are about 6 to 8 years old?

- physical skills – getting dressed, feeding themselves, drying off, etc.

- ability to swim – would be nice, but we can use a life vest.

- obedience – If they are out there in the water and they won't come back when you call, then you probably don't want them in the water, do you? If you ask them to clean up, they do.

- asking – they ask permission, they ask for things they want.

- service – they help others too

- intuition/conscience – knowing when they've gone too far, and listening to their conscience. What is right and wrong?

- being nice – not hitting other kids, they know how to play and how to make friends

- confidence – they don't just sit by you like a baby would; they go out and explore. They know they are loved.

Would they really have to know how to read or write?

Knowing their name and mom's name and number would be nice, but mostly for this age group, we would probably write it on their arm, or put a piece of tape with that info inside their swimsuit. Reading or writing would be nice, but it's not really a necessity, if you think about it.

That's what needs to be done in our homeschool first. We are building that foundation. Because as you can see with our beach day, we all need that beach to come back to. Now of course a beach is a sandy foundation, so that's one place where this analogy breaks down a bit. But our families do need a consistent foundation they can count on, and that should be the focus when our kids are young. That doesn't mean they can't learn to read and write; they certainly can, but it shouldn't be the focus. If you didn't set up your foundation when your kids were young, it's ok. You can still be building it!

For the next age group of children, about ages 7 to 11, the situation changes a bit. We noticed that with the little kids, they are all drawn to the water, and they want to explore. When kids get to ages 7 or so they are much more independent with what they can do. They can do so much more, and we let them go in the water because we know (or at least hope) they will obey and follow enough rules to be safe. They still always have the beach to come back to.

In this stage, our kids are exploring, venturing out a bit. This is a time for fun! When they aren't having fun, they'll pop back in to the beach. They are exploring and figuring things out. They are thinking and learning. If you watch kids this age playing, their play is a lot about real life. This helps them understand their life and how they fit into it better. I remember one time there was a heated political race going on in our community. Apparently we'd been talking about the candidates quite a bit, because one day I found my 7-year-old daughter playing with her Barbies, who happened to have the same names as those candidates! But it was her way of explaining what was going on around her.

Historically, this is the age when children begin more formal schooling, if it was even available. Preschool and kindergarten are rather modern inventions! It wasn't until 1873 that the first school district in America had a kindergarten, and by 1914, all major school systems had public kindergartens.

You could argue about whether or not this was a good idea as far as education goes, but it would also really depend on how the teaching in the kindergarten was structured. Early on, educational, reformers such as Friedrich Froebel who started the first kindergarten in Germany suggested that children are naturally good learners and that they learn through play. While kids still play in kindergarten, they have progressively become more academically based and play has become more limited.

Before this era of industrialization and World War I, small children would usually be at home with their mothers and families. It was the era of industrialization and World War I which created more working mothers and the difficulty of childcare, and popularized sending small children to public schools and preschoolers much sooner.

A school is defined as institution for educating children. It comes from the Greek word, *skholē*, which means "leisure, philosophy, place where lectures are given."

Interestingly, leisure means "use of free time for enjoyment," which is from the Latin word, "licere" or "be allowed." Philosophy means "the study of the fundamental nature of knowledge, reality, and existence" from Greek *philosophia* 'love of wisdom.'

Wisdom means "the quality of having experience, knowledge, and good judgment."

That is an interesting study on the word 'school'. The Greeks believed it was a time and place to be allowed to learn. In modern times, we could also allow our kids to enjoy learning as they think about their world, other people and how they themselves fit into the world. Learning and thinking are key!

Learning is defined as "to gain or acquire knowledge of or skill in (something) by study, experience, or being taught."

Thinking is to "direct one's mind toward someone or something; use one's mind actively to form connected ideas."

In education, you start off learning skills and knowledge, preferably when you are ready to learn.

Once you have a few basic skills, you can use those skills to learn more, to create, to apply it to yourself and to share what you know. For example, once you've learned the basic skill of reading, you can read more to learn, you can read directions to create things, you can read to find out more about yourself and your world, and you can teach others about what you've read or the skill of reading.

This is a pattern for education, where you learn like this:

1. Learn skills and knowledge

2. Use skills and knowledge to create. You must think to create.

3. Connect skills and knowledge to other skills and knowledge to apply the information. Connecting also requires thinking.

4. Share what you know with others—teach others, help others!

This isn't a direct path, meaning you don't have to perfectly complete #1 before going to #2. That's because you may have some knowledge in an area that you could create and connect and share with others, even if you don't know everything first. You don't have to be an expert. This is more like a cycle you just keep on repeating.

A skill is the ability to do something. If you're skilled at something, you can do it well. The only way to get a skill is to either be born naturally talented at it or to practice it. Of course if someone who is naturally talented doesn't practice, they won't get any better at it. If someone isn't naturally talented at something, it doesn't mean they can't develop that skill—it just means they'll need more dedication.

In the 7 to 11 age range, we focus on developing skills and gaining knowledge, and learning to love learning. Love of learning is different than entertaining. While we were on the beach, we didn't entertain the kids whole time. They wouldn't have wanted us to because they'd want to be free to explore. Nor would we want to be entertaining them the entire time.

They were gaining knowledge and skills as they explored the beach. They learned about how things work in their world around them, and they also learned skills. Swimming is a skill. Some kids take to swimming like fish in water; for others it's more of a struggle. But with enough practice, they can all learn to swim. Of course I'm talking about most people; clearly some people may have physical disabilities that may prevent that, but even still, look at Nic Vujicic. He was born with no legs or arms but he can swim! It may just take some people longer than others, but they can learn skills.

In our homeschool, it is during these middle years (ages 7-12 or so) that we keep building the foundation but also start to focus on learning academic skills and knowledge. That doesn't mean academics couldn't be taught earlier on; it just means it's more of a focus now. It also doesn't mean that you stop teaching the skills of the earlier stage.

Ok, I know you can teach a kid how to swim by throwing them in the water (being ready to jump in if they are drowning). Sometimes you may even have to do that, but I think that is for more extreme circumstances, or perhaps certain personalities. Plus it's much easier to wait until they are ready! A baby isn't really ready to learn math facts. Some kids may be ready at age 3, others maybe not until 10 or 12.

One of my sons was really not ready to learn how to write, so if he ever had things he wanted to say, I just wrote it down for him. He simply wasn't ready. In 10th grade, he jumped in the lake not knowing how to swim, figuratively speaking, when he chose to take a college English course. With a great teacher and support from home, he learned how to write, and write well, very quickly.

Sometimes we think we have to make our kids learn things. We can see they could do it and maybe we think they are lazy or going to be failures because we aren't doing our job. But it's so much easier if they are willing to learn. It's so much better if they are allowed to learn on their timeline. I have kids who are so willing to learn whatever I introduce to them. Then I have a couple of kids in particular who if they think I want them to learn something, boy, they do not want to. So that's when I choose the "I believe you'll learn it when you're ready" method.

For example, I had a 7.5-year-old son who had no interest in learning to read. I would offer periodically, but I had to totally take an "I don't care if you do or not" attitude or else he would dig in his heels and never choose it.

Mostly he didn't, but on occasion he would. I created an environment where he knew what skills were important to have. We are a reading family! We read aloud, we have lots of books, we listen to books, we read over here. He started believing that maybe he was dumb because he compared himself to his friends in public school, but I told him that he wasn't. I knew that for sure. I just knew he was going to read when he wanted to.

One day, he came to me with a book that he thought looked so awesome. It had a cool hero in a cape, holding up his sword in the air. Yes, it was a 1500-page novel. He says to me, 'Mom, I really want to read this."

I replied, "Okay, buddy. That sounds great! But maybe you'd better learn to read first." After that, he willingly did his reading lessons for about five weeks. Guess what happened. Because he was ready and willing, he learned to read at about a 4th or 5th grade level in those five weeks. Clearly not all kids will progress at that rate, but it shows the power of ready and willing—and it being HIS idea! Now he loves to read.

Just like when the kids are playing in the lake, they are going to enjoy it a lot more if I'm not out there directing their every move. I could have made them do an hour of swimming lessons, then an hour of kayaking lessons, if we'd had time. But instead, I can give them boundaries (like don't go too far out in the water and wear a life jacket); I can give them resources (a kayak or a raft) and then let them go. They will still learn.

If they already had swimming lessons and knew how to swim, this would be easy. If they didn't, they can still learn and have fun and connect with their cousins. At the beach, we provided kayaks, and the directive of wearing life jackets. But we didn't give them swimming lessons because that wasn't really the point of the day or the place to practice. My 7-year-old had never been in a kayak, but she had observed others. She had no fear, she hopped in and took off, and turns out, she's a natural at it. She didn't even need lessons at all! Now if she wanted to get better and be a pro, maybe we'd get her some instruction. But to start off, which is what we're doing in this phase, we just need to give boundaries, resources, direction and skills and then let them have at it. But we aren't ignoring them! During this age, I want my kids to LOVE learning.

What were the oldest kids doing on the beach? The teens (about ages 12+) were pretty independent. They knew the rules, and they had the skills for the most part to swim and enjoy the day. They would return to the foundation for food, to take a break, or on occasion if they had a question or needed help.

That is just like it should be in homeschool. Teens should be moving towards mostly being independent because in a few short years mom won't be there anymore to keep them on track! As you empower your teens to be more and more self-directed, you're freeing your time up and training them to be responsible adults as well.

Now, when your kids are around 12 or 13, you may have kids that make you think, "This kid is never going to get into college!" This is where I say hold your belief in that kid and keep on encouraging. That kid will do some amazing things that you never thought were possible. Really. I've seen it happen time and time again. Please stop worrying and trust that your kid will figure it out. For some the progress is gradual; for others, one day they wake up motivated and ready to do what it takes and they do!

As you allow your kids to try and fail in their more independent studies, they will get there. Now it may be that they didn't form those important skills in that first stage and they need more practice. If so, no problem! Have them practice. Consistency and doing what needs to be done is a difficult skill. (You probably know this for yourself!) If your child is struggling with that, it could be a personality thing (some personalities can be consistent much more than others, but all can learn it). It's not because you failed!

Another thing was that the teenagers were spending a lot more time away from the beach on more expensive equipment, such as the water trampoline or WaveRunners. In order for your kids to go farther in their education, they may need extra resources and opportunities as well, such as co-op classes, mentors, etc.

Around age 12-13, kids do need more. They may or may not have loved learning when they were younger, but this is when I start offering them bigger challenges. I want them to have bigger experiences that they can do on their own. I think about what they enjoy, keep my eyes open for new opportunities, or create them if I can't find them

Maybe you think there is nothing out there for homeschooled kids and they have to go to high school to get opportunities. But there is so much out there if you keep your mind open to it!

High school classes are only one option. My oldest daughter really wanted to do a study abroad, but most of them cost a lot of money, which wasn't really feasible then. One day, a homeschool mom who lived in Ecuador posted in a Facebook group asking for older teenage girls to come and live with her family as a nanny for three months. She would pay each month too, all the girl needed to do was to get there.

My first thoughts were, "Oh cool!" Then I went to, "Oh, but I don't know that person, and we don't have money for a plane ticket. That would be weird. That's for someone more adventurous." and so on...

Then I realized that a golden opportunity had opened up. Those were all just rationalizations that could be taken care of. That was fear speaking!

I contacted this woman and found that we actually had friends in common. We believed many of the same things. I felt good about the opportunity! I asked my daughter if she wanted to do it, and if she wanted to earn money for the plane ticket. She had some other things she wanted to do, but she felt like she really wanted to do it.

Once she decided, we had to figure out how a busy 16-year-old girl could earn $1,200 in two months. Except we didn't, because the very next day I saw an advertisement asking for newspaper delivery drivers. She took the job because it was one she could do during the early morning hours when she wasn't busy, and earned more than the needed amount before she left.

People who see opportunities and act on them get them. But it's hard to act because of the fear and the reasons your brain comes up with as to why you shouldn't. Those are the obstacles in your path on the hero journey. Get around them.

Some of you read my story and think, "Oh, that's nice for her. But I don't have time or money for that. I don't have opportunities like that. I don't have..." But I didn't either!

Here's another example. This same daughter was struggling with feeling grateful to live in a wonderful home with her wonderful family, and having to share her room with her little brother. I kept having the thought that she needed to go on a humanitarian trip to see how other people lived (oh and to serve of course!). I had no idea where to find that or how to do it. Many of the service trips I found looked great but I didn't know anything about who was running them, and they cost thousands of dollars. I prayed about it, kept my mind and eyes open. After a few months, I happened to run across an amazing man who arranged humanitarian trips around the world. I contacted him and I knew this was the path to take. I set up a trip for our co-op. The kids got to go to Mexico and serve for a week for only $500. I also helped the kids fundraise that money so they paid for it themselves. I did not know what

I was doing, but that didn't matter! When she got home, she saw our home much differently.

Basically, I keep my eyes open for opportunities that I think my kids might like. For one son, I saw a class being offered to learn how to repair bikes. I knew that son was mechanically inclined, so I signed him up! (I did ask him first.) After that class, he would repair bikes for kids in the neighborhood and get paid.

I bought my 10-year-old son a Rubik's Cube for Christmas. He didn't look at it for two months but that was fine. One night, his older brother's friends were talking about Rubik's Cubes and how they had learned to solve them. This impressed him so much that he learned how to solve a Rubik's Cube the next week.

My second oldest son liked the idea of construction. I heard about a class where he learned to build a house from the ground up! I had no idea that such a thing existed, but when I heard about it, I knew it would be great. My oldest son took a class on small engine repair. He and my next son started a lawn-mower repair business and made a lot of money. I could keep going, but you get the idea!

Not everything has to be big and amazing (for example, the Rubik's Cube opportunity was not!). But keep your eyes open and look for opportunities. Pay attention to your refusals. Can you get around those? Then commit to action and do it.

Another thing I've done is created "challenges" for kids who have a hard time getting motivated. I keep them completely requirement-free, but I let them know the opportunity is available. I encourage them to do it. For example, right now I have a daughter who doesn't like to practice math calculation skills. I gave her a challenge to be able to do 60 math facts in a minute, and if she can, she'll get $10. She's been practicing! But I don't make her do it.

I know the next question is this: How can I do this, when I don't have money to do challenges like that! The answer is, I budget for stuff like this! My kids are required to buy their own clothing, so that's how I have a budget for it—and why they are motivated. The money isn't there to make them do it, but rather to get them started.

Most people have no idea what they want out of life, even as adults! The way you find out is to just keep doing things, and having different experiences!

Of course quite often, teens are hesitant to do anything you want them to do. No problem. Ask them what they want to do. Require that they do something productive—they can choose, or you will. I give ideas and share opportunities, and sometimes my kids want to, and sometimes they don't. Which is fine! My daughter really wanted to go to cosmetology school, and that wasn't even on my radar! But she didn't figure that out until she'd had a lot of other experiences first.

This whole beach/education analogy matches up with what many leading psychologists and homeschool theories have taught about these stages. For example, in Jean Piaget's theory of cognitive development, he breaks up stages of development for children as follows:

Birth to 2: Infants are only aware of what is in front of them. They focus on what they see, what they are doing.

Ages 2 to 7: Children begin to be able to think symbolically, but their thinking is all based on intuition and not totally logical yet. They develop memory and imagination so they can begin to understand the concept of time.

Ages 7 to 12: Children begin developing logical reasoning, and they begin to think more of things around them and not so much about themselves. They still can't totally think abstractly.

Ages 13 to adult: Children start to think in more abstract terms. They start to think about relationships and ideological concepts.

Classical Education – this type of education returns to the ancient Greek and Roman form of education. It's based on the trivium, which includes three phases of learning.

Grammar stage (grades 1 to 4 or K to 6, ages 5 to 12): During these years, children begin learning knowledge through facts and memorizing.

Logic stage (grades 5 to 8 or 7 to 8, ages 12 to 14): Children focus on thinking, logic and questioning why

Rhetoric (grades 9 to 12, ages 14 to 18): This is the time for children to learn how to creatively express ideas and opinions through communicating (speaking and writing).

In the public school system, it is divided into these sections:

Early Childhood Education (age 3 to 6): The focus is on learning through play (In the beginning it was an academic focus that is "fun," but it's changed to more academic focus.)

Primary education (age 7 to 13): Children are to develop critical thinking and logic, and to enjoy learning.

<u>Secondary education (age 14 to 18):</u> Children begin a course of rigorous academic courses and electives.

In the book, *A Thomas Jefferson Education*, Oliver DeMille describes the phases of learning people go through. Ages are approximate, and many adults may find that they are still in the beginning phases.

<u>Core phase – ages 0 to 8:</u> the time to establish core values, good habits and learn about relationships.

<u>Love of Learning phase – ages 8 to 12:</u> the time to explore options, discover your talents and learn to love learning.

<u>Transition phase – ages 12 to 14:</u> the time to start learning study skills and beginning to become more of a serious scholar

<u>Scholar phase – ages 14 to 18:</u> a time of intense study, guided by a mentor.

<u>Depth scholar phase – ages 18 to 25:</u> time of very intense study, also guided by a mentor

<u>Mission phase</u> – time to change the world by doing good, using your knowledge, skills and experience.

Charlotte Mason was a 17th-18th century educator in England who was the founder of another popular educational philosophy. Her method is also sometimes called "the gentle art of learning." She recommended a gentle approach in the early years and more structured learning in later years. For younger children she was a great advocate of "living books" rather than textbooks, and also recommended a lot of outdoor time, doing hands-on activities and providing a rich learning atmosphere.

While all these philosophies differ from one another, they also agree in many areas. The stages of learning are all essentially the same when it comes to child development.

CHAPTER 18

Lighting the Fire

One of my favorite quotes comes from WIlliam Butler Yeats:

"Education is not the filling of a bucket but the lighting of a fire."

Filling the bucket is the gaining knowledge part. But unless the fire is lit, what is all that knowledge good for?

Without a love of learning, our kids are just learning to be obedient puppies. When you love learning, you'll keep on learning and it's so exciting! But when you're just learning for a test or because someone said you had to, you'll default to doing the minimum and eventually you just don't care.

Many of my son's friends who could read before he could actually hate to read. They rarely will do it for enjoyment! I think that's partly because they weren't ready for the skill when they learned it, so they associated reading with "a lot of work" rather than something they could love. But it's also partly because reading is often required, so kids will do the minimum amount to get by.

How do you light the fire?

Have fun – Enjoy yourselves, don't get into power struggles! Don't stress out over trying to make your kids learn! They will! Also, think about this: Having fun is different from providing entertainment.

Be passionate and have enthusiasm – Get excited about what you're doing. What if you're not excited about anything? It's a choice. It really is! Even if you don't have any interest in something, you can choose enthusiasm.

Create good feelings – Ok, so maybe this is just a repeat of the first two. But this is so important that I'm saying it again. When you're learning, intentionally create good feelings around your learning times! If you feel good, you want to keep doing it!

<u>Ask questions / have discussions</u> – Talk about what you're learning together. Don't have right or wrong answers, just discuss. Let everyone share their opinions and make them feel like their viewpoints are just as valid as anyone else's.

<u>Make connections</u> – When you can connect what you're learning to something in your everyday life, it will make more sense and it will stick with you longer. Master teachers will use this method to compare concepts to things that are familiar. When the learners come up with analogies like this, not only will they remember what they are learning for a longer time, but learning becomes exciting!

<u>Play and acting things out</u> – Children learn so much from play. It's where they're making sense of their world; they can act out things in a safe environment. It also fosters a lot of creativity. Adults can learn a lot from play too!

<u>Share what you're learning with others</u> – As you teach what you've learned, you'll understand it so much better. It also helps you become more excited about topics as you share what you've learned.

<u>Surround with greatness</u> – Surround others with ideas of their own greatness and potential so they feel inspired to want to do and become more than they currently are. Share stories of great people and let them know they aren't any different. They can do this too.

<u>Believe in them</u> – Don't forget who your children really are, the good they have inside and the greatness they can become! This is especially important when they aren't acting that like the good people they are inside. Treat them as the amazing people they are inside and can become. Don't forget this for yourself either.

<u>Offer unconditional love</u> – Love them no matter what. We are all humans, so we can't have perfect unconditional love, but we can practice loving our kids more and more every day, no matter how they are acting. They don't have to earn our love. When someone feels loved, they feel like they can change.

<u>Provide a safe environment in which to learn</u> – Because your kids know they are loved no matter what, they can see it's OK to fail and to make mistakes. They can learn from these things. If someone feels shamed or judged when they aren't living up to your expectations, it's going to be difficult to be inspired to want to learn or to become better; it's easier just to give up if they can't ever get to the perfection they think they need to attain to gain your approval.

The other day I was teaching a class, and one of the boys made a mistake in his math. I asked him to check his work again to see if he'd gotten the right answer. He was pretty sure it was right, but I told him I always double check my work because mistakes are easy to make. He did and he found out his answer was off. I praised his finding the mistake and fixing it. A few minutes later, he said to me, "I'm really embarrassed!" I asked him why. He replied that he was really good at math and he was so embarrassed that he had messed up. I assured him it was really no big deal. I told him I was really good at math too, but I mess up all the time; that's why I always double check my work! I assured him that he didn't need to feel embarrassed over making a mistake. He could still be good at math, and making mistakes was how we get better. He felt better after that, because it really wasn't a big deal. I still liked him and he didn't need to always be perfect at math to have my approval.

Inspire, not require – Many homeschoolers have heard of this concept and I think it's rather misunderstood. Inspire is really all about lighting the fire, getting the kids excited to learn. Typically when you require people to do things, they will do the minimum amount possible to get by. That's why I will avoid requiring school work whenever possible. However, while this phrase is very catchy, it doesn't mean that you should never require. While kids are younger, I'm going to require a lot less by way of school work. But I am going to require that they are obedient and that they do their chores. As the kids get older, they will have more requirements in some areas, and less in others. They are required to always have someone with them when on the computer. They may be required to report in to me every week about what they are doing. They may be required to consistently turn in assignments to a class.

But just because someone is required to do something doesn't mean they always do it. Whether they do or don't, they will have a consequence (good or bad). And it's ok! If they don't do something, they can learn from that, and I don't need to make them feel bad about it.

We light the fire by inspiring them to want to be better and to do what it takes to become better, and we don't put the fire out by crushing them when they don't live perfectly!

Ideally we'd love it if our kids were always motivated internally (feeling inspired) but sometimes using external motivators is really useful to get them moving. But if you do use a reward, you can't attach it to your approval. You have to let them choose to do it or not!

CHAPTER 19

Am I Doing Enough?

As moms, we do tend to get worried. Am I covering enough? Am I failing my kids? What if…

You know what I mean. We've all done it before, and we all do it now. We want our kids to succeed because they are awesome and amazing, they are full of potential! But as homeschool moms we've taken on a BIG responsibility—not only are we raising them, but we also have taken responsibility for their education.

That's like saying you're taking full responsibility for your kids to have a good time on the lake. Well, what if they get sunburnt even though you applied sunscreen (or maybe even you didn't). Can they still have a good time? Sure. But you can't make them. What if they get mad because the other kids won't play with them or all the Cheetos are taken? Could they still choose to have a good time? Sure. But you can't make them.

You can try, but we all know you can't make your kid have a good time if they don't choose to. You can distract, console, comfort, all that. But ultimately, you know it's up to your kids to choose if they have a good time or not. In the lake setting, it's pretty easy to have fun.

Same thing with their education. You can send them to school, you can homeschool them. But you can't make them learn. You can't make them like it. You can't make them lead out and get educated. You can't make that horse you led to water drink if it isn't thirsty.

Please don't take responsibility for your children's education. That is not your responsibility. What you took on when you decided to homeschool was to take responsibility to create the environment in which they could choose to take responsibility for their education. Why is that important? Because that is something you can mostly control. It's scary to allow your kids to take responsibility for their own education—what if they don't choose it?

You have to stand firm in the belief that your child is inherently good and wants to be and do good. Because it's true! Where you get messed up is when you child does something that's not in line with who he really is. Then you blame yourself instead of realizing that this child is an amazing human being who isn't perfect but still learning and growing.

How do you do that? How do you encourage your kids to take responsibility for their own education by creating the environment? This is where you've got the power, ladies! It's all the things I've been talking about in this book:

- Believing in your children's goodness and greatness

- Training your children to have good character (which just means to act like the good person you are, even when it is hard)

- Giving them boundaries to keep them safe

- Creating a feeling of acceptance, love and lack of shame in the home

- Having a great relationship with your kids

- Allowing them to grow on their timeline, not mine or others

- Setting the example

- Believing in your intuition

- Managing how I react to situations

- Taking responsibility for myself and my education

- Having order, systems, habits and routines in the home (that's coming up in the next part)

All of that is more important than the academics. Seriously. If you can focus on that, and put in maybe an hour a day on academics, your kids will choose ownership on their timeline. If you can believe this, you won't be able to stop your kids from taking ownership of their education in ways you never even dreamed of. I never thought my daughter would choose to get a cosmetology certificate. I did know she felt empowered to follow her dreams. I never thought my son who could barely write a few sentences at age 14 would be writing amazing college-level ten-page papers by age 16 and also would have read hundreds of great books. I did know that he would learn at his pace though. I never knew my oldest son would get his entire college career paid for with scholarships or that he'd move home from a good full-time job to start his own business. I did know he was destined to do some great things. The kids who take longer to figure out how to take responsibility for their own educations will help build your character as you strive to create your environment.

All of this is easier said than done. But it is worth it to do, and it makes your life a lot less stressful.

CHAPTER 20
Choosing Curriculum

When someone begins homeschooling, inevitably, the first thing they do is to ask this question:

"Help! I don't know where to start! What curriculum should I choose? What is the best curriculum? "

I started off this way too, but it's really not the best place to start. It's OK if you started this way too, I didn't know this either. It's not all about the curriculum!

Really, before you start home education, it's better to get a foundation of what education really is and why you are homeschooling your kids.

"Why" is what I've been trying to cover in this whole book. If you understand this philosophy of education, it narrows down the curriculum issue a lot, because much of it you just don't need.

"How" is also part of the philosophy, but not specific. Specific "how" is the curriculum.

Based on this philosophy of education, here is my philosophy of choosing curriculum:

For little kids, you don't really need curriculum. You just need to love them, work with them and play with them. Read good books and get workbooks if they like them, but don't make them do them.

For middle kids, the curriculum you choose really doesn't matter if you use it to guide their love of learning rather than allow it to guide you into misery. This is what I mean: If you miss a couple of weeks, and you feel panicked that you're behind, you're allowing it to guide you.

Here are my other guidelines:

- It should be engaging so the kids are happy when you say you're going to use it. Stories, music, games and activities are how kids stay engaged.

- It shouldn't take all day, because kids really need free time!

- If you have multiple kids, teach them all together or you'll go nuts. Like seriously crazy burnout.

- It shouldn't be too complicated or require complicated things, or you won't do it.

- It should spark interest and not necessarily give them all knowledge.

- It should be history-based, using stories, not just facts

- It should use great books when possible.

- It teaches good values and principles.

For teenagers, in addition to the guidelines above (with perhaps less hands-on, games and activities), I like to choose curriculum that they can study on their own. Reading and writing about great books is excellent, and I choose real books over textbooks whenever possible. I also love to involve my teens in co-op classes and they like this too as it gives them this added layer of accountability.

For all of us curriculum junkies: Many of us buy entirely way too much and then don't use it. Is that you? How do you feel about that?

I certainly have purchased a lot of curriculum in my last 18 years of homeschooling! For a long time I felt really guilty about not using most of it. I bet you know that feeling too. "Oh I wasted money on this." or "I'm such a slacker, I should be using this..." etc.

I finally realized that I am not a bad person who wasted money or is lazy simply because I bought curriculum I didn't use. I could learn from all those curriculum purchases! I could learn that it wasn't my kid's style, or that it didn't turn out as good as I hoped, and that is OK. I could learn academics and how to teach from it, even if I didn't actually use it with my kids. I learned my teaching style, after I learned I didn't have one yet, but the curriculum helped me figure it out. I learned that I didn't have enough discipline to actually teach my kids which didn't mean I had to send them back to school; it just meant I had to learn to get disciplined.

One problem with purchasing too much curriculum is that a part of us really thinks we are going to use it. We also tend to plan to teach way more than is realistically going to happen. I think that's partly because we get so excited, but partly because we fear we won't cover everything. Whatever you've planned for homeschool, you probably need to just let yourself know that if you get 50% of it done, you're doing great. If you only get 50% of that 50% done, you're still doing awesome.

CHAPTER 21

Fitting Homeschool in Your Day

Most of us spend way too long homeschooling (or thinking we need to do more). We're either teaching too much, or we're planning too much and then not teaching it because we spent so much time planning it that we don't have time to teach or we planned so much it seems overwhelming!

Personally, I only directly homeschool my kids for about an hour a day. We have a family learning time, which is awesome because I can commit to that. During this time, we cover all sorts of general knowledge, hands-on activities and read-alouds. They don't get bored and neither do I. I know I can fit it in because it won't take all day, and it's definitely a sanity saver.

I can homeschool in only an hour a day because I know my kids are on their own hero journeys and will love learning. When I know that I cover all the basics in that hour and I can end while they are still enjoying it, I'm not worried about making them do all their curriculum and pushing them to hating it.

You can see how you could fit homeschool in your day if it's only an hour a day, right?

But that doesn't mean that after that hour you're done. You're still putting in the time to:

1. Create that environment where they can learn and grow.

2. Focus on character training / consistency.

3. Lead the way – what do you need to do to get unstuck?

4. Build the belief that they are good, and have potential greatness inside. This is actually your #1 priority.

You can also create more time in your day by:

1. Creating more free space in your schedule by cutting down on outside activities insofar as possible. Kids need free time to learn too!

2. Knowing that it's OK to take a break from schooling and still homeschool. Your kids won't stop learning, I promise! When you have those periods of transition like moving, new baby, etc, give yourself a break. Go into minimum mode and build relationships with your kids, let them play, or read a book to them.

3. Realizing that you don't have to teach your kids every single thing they need to know. They will learn. Take the pressure off yourself, because if you feel like you have to homeschool for six hours a day, it's very possible you are using your kids to prove your own worth and to avoid being a "failure" based on their performance. That's a lot of pressure on them and you.

4. Creating systems to keep the household running smoothly. That's the next section!

When I first started homeschooling, the house was a disaster because I was spending so much time on homeschooling. It's hard to learn in chaos! We need the order too!

Then the pendulum swung way over in the other direction, and I would spend time trying to get the house in order and never get around to homeschooling!

That can make a person crazy.

There had to be a balance. Part of that was to consistently choose to homeschool for just an hour a day because that was doable. The other part was to discipline myself to follow a system.

PART 3
CLEAN THE HOUSE

CHAPTER 22

Your Perfect Home Depends on YOU!

A few weeks ago, I got an email with this subject line: YOUR PERFECT HOME DEPENDS ON YOU!

I thought, Wow! That's pressure! Then I thought, "Wow, no wonder we feel stressed out with messages like this bombarding us on all sides. I have to have a perfect home and it all depends on me!" No wonder we're all going crazy!

So let me just tell you, girl, you don't need a perfect home. Plus who are you kidding? You have kids at home messing up things all.the.time; you homeschool!

An orderly home would be nice, to be sure.

My goal is to have my systems in place well enough so that I can get the house clean in 15-20 minutes at any given time. So in a sense, your clean home does depend on you, on you putting in systems and making them work so that you can have a clean home.

You get to decide your stress level of the cleanliness of your house. Do you want a lived-in home or a museum? Too much clutter and dirt can cause serious stress. But on the flip side, a perfect home can cause serious stress just trying to keep it that way. I have a friend who kept her home so clean, her kids weren't even allowed to sit on the couch!

So you decide, what is your basic maintenance plan? Is it OK to have messy closets and areas of your house that aren't always totally organized? I definitely have areas of my house I wouldn't want to bring guests in, but my main living areas are clean and inviting. I allow the kids to make messes and I allow them to clean them up too (more imperfectly than I would!).

CHAPTER 23

Principles and Systems

Do you know the difference between a principle and a system? I didn't understand this for a long time, but once I learned this, it helped me so much with making decisions in my life.

The word principle comes from the Latin word that means "source or foundation." The dictionary defines it as "a fundamental truth or proposition that serves as the foundation for a system of belief or behavior or for a chain of reasoning"

Basically, a principle is a foundational idea that is true.

Throughout this book, I've talked about finding patterns in life to make life more predictable, more stable, more secure, and more successful. What I'm really talking about is finding principles that are true. True principles are ones that are true for everyone and are repeatable. They match natural law, and they bring greater freedom to your life. For example, continual learning is a true principle because it makes our lives better as we keep on learning.

Finding those true principles is what we're really doing as we go along our hero journeys. The more true principles we can find, the more predictable our life is, and the easier our journey becomes, because we can get around the obstacles more quickly.

It is fascinating to try to determine what true principles are. One way I do this is that I think of a topic I want to know more about—usually because I'm struggling with it. I look up the meaning of the word and the word etymology to see if that gives me any more clarity. Then I will write out a list of what I think are true principles. I will then test those principles in my own life to see if they are true. One concept I did this with was the principle of order. I had struggled with keeping my house clean! I decided I needed to learn about the principle of order. The next chapter will show you how I did this.

A system is simply a way to implement those principles in your life. There can be many different systems that can all achieve the same results, using the same principles, but in different ways.

For example, continual learning can be done by taking classes in your community, reading books, listening to audiobooks, taking online classes, getting a mentor, etc. Those are all just systems that supports the principle of continual learning.

Many of the things I've talked about in this book are principles of education. I've also suggested many different systems to help you use these principles. See if you can tell what they are and what the difference is. You may or may not agree with the principles of education, but in my experience they have held true. You won't know for sure unless you test the principles out yourself. But also realize that just because a system may not work for you doesn't mean the principle is incorrect.

Typically if I find a principle I believe to be true because I've seen successful people using it or I've read about it, I may need to test it with different systems until I get the results I am expecting.

Where people get confused is between principles and systems. A system is simply how you do something. In general, there aren't systems that are true for everyone. A certain system may work well for someone else, but maybe not work for you. It can be based on a true principle or not. Where it gets confusing is that often you don't know what principle you are following or what end result you want. So while continual learning may be a true principle, there are a lot of systems to make that happen. We may think about educational systems, but perhaps each system defines education differently and thus the systems may not bring about more freedom or success to life.

Think first about what principle you are trying to accomplish when creating a system. Also look at why you are creating that system.

CHAPTER 24

Principles of Order

Through the years I have seriously struggled with keeping order in my home. I would get so frustrated and think I was just no good at it! Periodically, I would get determined to make a change. I would spend hours creating a new system. This time I would overhaul everything and get it right! I would write out exactly what I wanted to do, complete with cute graphics, colors and lamination. This would make me so excited to try it out!

But inevitably, I would get it all ready to go, try it out for a few days, and then it would fall by the wayside. And I would have another failure under my belt.

I was stuck in this depressing cycle for such a long time! I felt like I was never going to make progress! I'm a reasonably intelligent person, I thought. But why couldn't I figure this out? And it's not like I'm trying to get to the moon; all I wanted was a little order. How could I get there?

Isn't that what we all want? It feels good to have and create order! I knew that! I remember one day, I spent all day cleaning out my pantry. It looked amazing! When you walked in, everything was all in line and orderly. Each item was categorized in its own section. There were no old cereal bags with a ¼ cup of crushed cereal in there, no knocked-over boxes, no trash lying on the floor, no supplement bottles from 2002, no rancid noodles, no cans of garbanzo beans that no one was ever going to eat. Only lovely, beautiful order.

As I stood admiring my pantry, there was a knock at the door. There was my sister. You all know what I did next. Of course! I invited her to come take a tour of my pantry! She oohed and aahed as a good sister would do, and I felt thrilled that my newly found order was thrilling to her too.

Of course, just two days later, the pantry wasn't in perfect order anymore. Kids dropped stuff on the floor and left it there. I went shopping and didn't quite put it all away. A box of cereal was returned empty to the pantry.

As time went on, it got more frustrating. You know the feeling! You work hard to clean and organize something, but it doesn't stay that way.

I really wanted to figure this out. I began to ponder and study about order. I asked myself, "What are the principles of order that I need to know to have more order in my life?"

This isn't a complete list, but I wanted to share some of the principles of order that I believe to be true. But only because I have tested them. You have probably never thought about order in this way before, but you can test these ideas out too and come up with your own list of principles.

<u>Disorder and chaos are the natural state of life</u>

Everything in nature, if left unattended, returns to chaos. You could say that the natural state of nature is to move to disorder.

This clearly happens to my pantry every time I get it organized. I have a sister-in-law who has the most amazing pantry I've ever seen. (And yes, she showed it to us!) But even hers will move to disorganized if she doesn't keep up on it.

This happens in nature too! Think about a garden. Have you ever planted your garden in the spring, excited for the bounty in the fall, but after about a month you just stop working in it. We all know what happens next; it gets full of weeds. If you don't water it, the plants die but you know those weeds will still grow!

Got any flat surfaces in your house? Unless you're dusting regularly, you know what happens. Yep, covered with dust. Oh yes, and people will place things on the flat surfaces too and then more and more will collect.

Even human beings have a natural state that tends to return to chaos and disorder if left unchecked. The natural state of human feelings is to move to chaotic feelings such as anger, overwhelm or confusion.

In physics, there is the concept of entropy, which basically means there is a lack of order or predictability, things naturally gradually decline into disorder.

This is a well-established law of nature. But just because something is "natural" doesn't mean it's always the best. Nature takes the path of least resistance, it's where everything goes unless something happens to redirect or change it. Of course this also doesn't mean that "natural" or nature is bad. It only gets that label if we attach that meaning to it. A mess isn't bad. It is natural. Thus we don't need to be upset over a mess, but at the same time, we don't necessarily want to keep it that way.

<u>Human beings desire order</u>

I like things being in order! I don't always like putting the things into order, just because my brain says "Why even bother, it'll just get messed up again." But as humans, we really do like and even crave order in our lives.

Why is that? Why do you want order in your life?

When I was cleaning the pantry, at first it was just because I was sick of it being a mess.

I wanted to be able to find things.

I only wanted to store things that I would actually use.

I wanted to have room to put new groceries away.

I really just wanted the peace and calm that comes from having order.

When I was finished, I also wanted that proud feeling that I could create order out of chaos.

When I thought this through, I realized something. Creation is really just creating order out of disorder, creating something good that wasn't there before.

A quote I had heard not too long before came into my mind:

"The desire to create is one of the deepest yearnings of the human soul. No matter our talents, education, backgrounds, or abilities, we each have an inherent wish to create something that did not exist before." Everyone can create. You don't need money, position, or influence in order to create something of substance or beauty.

"Happiness, Your Heritage" Ensign, Nov 2008, Dieter F. Uchtdorf

We want order because we desire to create something better in our lives!

But because of natural law, we will never have everything perfectly in order or organized in this life. So we desire order, but there is always something out of order.

My pantry will always keep getting messy.

Order is related to our feelings

The natural reaction to my pantry getting messy after I spent all day cleaning it is to feel frustrated.

My heart's desire is to have order in my pantry!

This makes me feel conflicted! I want to feel happy and having order makes me feel more happy and peaceful, but it can never stay that way.

So I feel frustrated, and I get mad that I have to clean it out again.

After I clean it out, I feel happy. But then it happens all over again.

This is a vicious cycle we get trapped in.

And of course, this disorganization isn't just my pantry. It's all around me. My emotions keep going up and down like a roller coaster, and that's an exhausting, hard way to live!

No wonder it's hard to change.

When I was a kid, I was often angry. I didn't like being that way, and I felt like everyone thought I was mean. One day my brave mother suggested to me that I try smiling a little more. I say brave because of course I got angry at that suggestion. But I did try it. I found that I did have a little more control over my feelings than I thought I did.

As I got older, I learned that feelings didn't come because of how things were around me. They came because of how I thought things were around me. I found that I could change my thoughts which would change how often I felt angry. If I chose to look at my world with different thoughts that would make me happy, I would feel happier.

I'd heard that quote "It's nice to be important, but it's more important to be nice." and it's variation "It's more important to be nice than it is to be right." But what if I really was right? What if what I was thinking was the truth? I really couldn't reconcile this quote in my brain.

Not until I learned something key about emotions was I able to understand the quote more fully. Our emotions are neither good or bad. Sure, some of those emotions can feel negative or positive to us. But they aren't what makes us good or bad. They are simply a measurement tool. A thermometer isn't good or bad, but it can measure hot or cold, and we can interpret the temperature as negative or positive.

Our emotions are really only a measurement of how much our thoughts are in alignment with truth and who we really are. If I am feeling angry about something, then what I am thinking is not correct or true. I am getting a signal that something needs to change. I either need to change my thoughts or my actions to get myself back on track.

If I'm getting frustrated about my pantry getting messed up again, I can totally believe that I am right in thinking this, because it is frustrating!

But it is also natural law, and it will keep happening.

Order and disorder are to allow us a choice

What am I going to do with that frustration?

This is an obstacle on our hero's journey! Opposites, such as order and disorder, were given to us in this life because often it is the choices that are our obstacles on our path.

It is in the conflict that we have a choice, and it is in the conflict that we get the opportunity to grow.

Usually what happens is people hit this wall of frustration and give up. Why even bother to clean the pantry, when it's just going to get messed up again? Either that, or they take their frustrations out on those around them and blame them for the mess.

The thing is, you're just going to keep hitting that wall because you're not learning from it.

Once you recognize the obstacle is there, you can make a choice. You can keep hitting it by choosing to be frustrated every single time you walk in the pantry, or you can get around it by realizing that frustration is there to give you the clue that you are hitting the wall, and now you have an opportunity to learn!

You get to choose how long you keep running into that wall. You can't necessarily choose if you're going to run into the wall, but you can choose how long you let those negative feelings stay. But first you've got to figure out that you're hitting it. It's the negative feelings that come up for you that show you that you are hitting a wall. If you keep running into it for too long, you move off your hero journey path, and onto the path to disorder and chaos.

How do you get around that wall? How do you make a new choice? Is the way I look at disorder really a choice?

<u>Getting frustrated does not create the order you crave</u>

"Who threw this here? Why did you put this back in the pantry; that's so dumb! Why are you kids so messy?" I've thought and said things like this. Did it motivate my kids to be neater?

Uh, not really. Maybe if I get mad enough they will start cleaning, but it's out of fear, not out of a good desire to create more order.

The frustration is there because I don't have the order I crave. It's not because my kids are messy (well, that seems partly right), or because my husband or I are messy (that seems partly right too). The mess is there because that is natural law, and the frustration is there to show me I have an opportunity to become better.

I get to choose how long that frustration stays. I have choices! I could choose to:

1. Be frustrated every time I walk into the pantry.

2. Just clean it!

3. Get someone else to clean it.

4. Plan a different time to clean it later.

5. Choose to look at this disorder as an opportunity to learn and to create more order. Be excited at all the practice I will get.

6. Create a regular system to keep it clean and then discipline myself to do it. Maybe I will clean five things every time I walk in there.

7. Decide it's not worth worrying about and let it go, and then deep clean every six months.

What would you learn if you actually hit the wall and made a difference choice? How do you know what to do? What thoughts would make you feel happier?

Good things to think about!

<u>Physical order is a pattern for becoming</u>

As I started taking advantage of this idea that I had a choice, I started choosing to be grateful that I had so many opportunities to create more order! This is not easy. It's natural to be frustrated, but I had to check myself and say, "Hey! I have opportunities to create order! I am getting so much practice, I'm getting to be an expert at this!" when I caught myself feeling frustrated.

What I didn't realize was that creating order in my surroundings brought more order on the inside of me. As I recognized these negative emotions coming up that the chaos was triggering, I learned more to manage my emotions and I began to feel more calm.

Creating physical order is really just a pattern for us to create order within ourselves. Disorder in my life didn't mean that I was bad, sloppy, lazy or messy. It just meant that I had a lot of great opportunities for building my character, for developing self-discipline, for doing those things to move me along the path to becoming who I was meant to be!

I used to enjoy that quote that said, "A cluttered desk is the sign of a creative mind." If you look at that from the viewpoint that human beings are creative, and things go to their natural state, it could be true. But perhaps it is a rationalization.

A cluttered desk is really just a sign of a creative, undisciplined mind. It just means you didn't take the time or discipline yourself to clean it. An organized desk is the sign of a creative, organized mind. If you have a clean desk, your brain will be much less cluttered too, and you can be more creative!

Human beings have an order

If you're like me, you probably have messes and areas you could go clean and organize. It is OK for those messes to wait for another day as long as they aren't so overwhelming you and your family can't function

This is good to recognize, because we don't have to do everything all now. There is a sequence in which each one of us may create order in our own lives.

As you start with changing one thing, you will start seeing improvement in the other areas of your life. Not as fast as you think it should be, but it will come. Begin with the one thing you are struggling with the most or the one thing that bothers you the most.

Consistency is key to keeping order

As you begin to become more consistent in small changes, you'll find that over time you've made big changes. Being consistent in the small things is more important than knowing how to get to the big change. Creating order requires discipline! Discipline is how you become who you are meant to be. You wouldn't struggle with something if you already knew how or could already do it. This is why it's such an awesome learning opportunity!

It doesn't really matter where you start, just that you do start. Start doing a small action consistently, and you'll know what you need to do next. Do all things in order; don't do things faster than you have strength.

Creating order is powerful

When things are orderly, you will feel more peaceful as well as have more energy in your life. When things are disorderly, you feel more overwhelmed and those negative feelings pop up more.

Creating order brings more power into your life, because you can control the order around you and how you feel about it. When you can discipline yourself to consistently create order, you feel more energy and light in your life.

I didn't know this at first either. I just knew I wanted ordered. As I was consistent in creating more order, I found this to be true.

Your example is the most powerful way to teach this to your children. You can try to use that frustration to motivate your kids to clean, but then they are just going to be frustrated over disorder. You can't force your kids but you can enforce your requests for obedience.

Let's say you have a messy house. You can start yelling at them to get this disaster clean. If you are mad enough they will clean. Afterwards though, you may have a clean house, but you will feel badly about how you handled that. Alternatively, you can ask that they clean up something specific. If they don't obey, you can calmly say, "I'm sorry you didn't obey when I asked you to do that, so now I will need to add on another chore so you can learn to obey."

Having a choice is what really empowers you in your life. You have a choice in how you look at the messes in your life. You can choose the natural state, the path of least resistance, and feel frustrated, but then you will start to beat yourself up:

"I'm such a mess! I can't get it together!"

Or you blame everyone else:

"They are such a mess, they never can keep anything in order."

Or you can choose the third choice:

"How awesome it is that I get to create order every day!" A hero chooses gratitude every chance she gets!

Oh, and your kids will like you this way a lot better.

CHAPTER 25

Systems of Order

Now you know one of my crazy secrets: that I choose to be grateful for disorder in my life! But I have two disclosures.

1. I have plenty of my own disorder so I don't need any more (so don't bother offering yours, you get to keep yours, it's specially designed for you!)

2. I don't always feel grateful and sometimes I still complain. But overall, the more I practice, the better I get at it and the happier I am. For most of us, this takes a lot of practice.

In fact, I've only run across one person who seems to have been born genuinely happy about messy rooms, and that would be Marie Kondo, author of *The Life-Changing Magic of Tidying Up*. It is probably why she is so appealing and maddening at the same time—she hits that inner conflict of frustration and desire for order right on the head!

Knowing these principles changes things, and it helps you choose new systems to create order.

Our homes and kids give us plenty of opportunities to get good at creating order.

You have systems to create order in your home now, whether you're aware of it or not, but they may not be the most efficient systems to keep your house mostly in order.

That's why you need to experiment with different systems to see what will work for you. But don't always blame the system either.

One of the biggest things to remember with any system is that you just need to do it. I used to spend hours creating these complicated systems that I could not keep up on and I just wasn't going to do it. So keep the system as simple as possible, and then when you said you'd do it, do it. Once it is a habit, you don't have to keep on deciding to do it.

Decide that you are a person who creates order, so that when the excuses come up about why you can't follow your system now, you remember that you are a person who creates order, so you make yourself do it anyway.

Let me give you an example of a system. Currently, I have all my kids over the age of eight do their own laundry. They each have their own day and so do I. Do they do it perfectly? Heavens no! But by the time they leave the house they are very comfortable with washing their own laundry. On my laundry day, I just get it done because I'm a person who creates order and I am so grateful I get to!

TIPS FOR STAYING ON TOP OF IT

(that probably all seem really obvious, but aren't always!)

1 – Clean as you go

My kids hear me say this all the time, but it really does work! While you are in the middle of a messy project (or making dinner), just take the time to clear and rinse and clean up and throw stuff away as you are doing it.

2 – Finish

Discipline yourself to finish your small jobs before walking away. For example, how often do you fold the laundry, but then you don't put it away? This actually just happened to me. I was washing the dishes and stacking. But I got bored, so I was about to go into the other room to do something else when I remembered that I like to tell myself, "I am a finisher!" So I spent maybe two minutes finishing the job and I proved to myself that was true! Notice if that's you – do you get so distracted and move on to something else without finishing? Change that!

3 – Make a five-minute cleanup habit

Periodically do five-minute cleanups throughout the day, or at least once a day! You'd be amazed at how much you can get done in 5 minutes. Set a timer and be done at five minutes, unless you consciously decide you want to keep cleaning; otherwise you will avoid five-minute cleanups in the future. Call to the kids to help too! "Okay, everyone is going to clean up for five minutes, starting now! If you don't feel like participating, that's fine, but then you get to clean for ten minutes by yourself!" That usually does the trick.

4 – Create morning and evening routines

A quick clean in the morning and evening will do wonders to stay on top of things. This is a great time to train your kids to do chores.

<u>5 – Always clean up after meals</u>

No one likes washing a sinkful of dishes with dried-on food, and my dishwasher sure can't handle that. It's wise to clean up after your meals soon after eating. Except when you can't. Then clean up as soon as possible.

<u>6 – Get multiple sets of cleaning supplies</u>

If it's not convenient, you're not going to do it. Keep a set of cleaning supplies in each room you need to use them in.

<u>7 – Never leave a room empty-handed</u>

Train yourself to see what is out in the room, and when you leave the room, bring something with you to put away. This is especially effective if you have stairs and people put stuff on a step to be brought up, but never do!

<u>8 – Decide fast and act</u>

A lot of the time we avoid doing things because we haven't decided what to do. Many times we haven't decided because we want to make sure we get the right answer. Remember, our brains want to be right! So we will put off making a decision simply because we don't know what the right answer is. We also fear making the wrong decision because we don't want to fail. When you avoid making a decision, it really takes a lot of energy out of you! Notice if you aren't making a decision simply because there isn't a right answer or you're afraid you'll fail. Most of the time, what you decide doesn't really matter.

A good example for this is when I first thought about homeschooling. I didn't know how, so I wasn't sure of what the right answer was. I didn't do anything for a long time. Then I started researching, and it was overwhelming because there is so much! I spent a very long time researching, which was helpful except that had I just chosen something and tried it out, I would have learned much more quickly what would work.

Often we get stuck in this mode where we believe we have to know everything about it first (we have to know the right answer) before we can do anything. This takes a lot more energy than learning enough, deciding to do something and then doing it. Yes, you might choose wrong, but that is how you learn.

<u>9 – Make Time to Plan</u>

I say to decide fast, but if you haven't taken the time to make plans first, it's going to be really hard to know what to decide. I have found that when I set aside time for mentally creating what I want, it's much simpler to decide fast and act on the right things.

There is a balance here. You can spend too much time in your head and never get anything done! On the flip side, if you don't take the time to think about what you really want, you can end up just running at full speed, trying to do every good thing that comes your way.

<u>10 – Just because you can, doesn't mean you should</u>

Homeschool moms are some of the most capable human beings I know! We can do so many different things. Just because we can, though, doesn't mean we should. We are also notorious for piling on the "shoulds" and then trying to do them all. This is why it's so important to know what it is you really want, so the shoulds don't weigh down your should-ers.

<u>11 – Do, delegate, or delete</u>

In the book, *Getting Things Done*, the author David Allen suggests that when you have tasks, you either do them right away, delegate them to someone else, or delete the task by deciding you don't need to do it. You can also delay tasks, but you need to consciously decide when you'll work on that later; otherwise your list will get full of all the things you delayed.

<u>12 – Make your bed</u>

Yes, make your bed every morning. Why? It really starts your day off right with "getting it done" energy! You will feel more motivated. It's also really nice to get into a nicely bed at night. If you get into your unmade bed, it's pretty likely you're going to get some thoughts in which you beat yourself up for being a slob. "Bed-making" is a great training for your kids, and they can do it (albeit not as nicely as you) when they are very young. Some kids catch on really fast and will be quite consistent. Others, like me, will take years and years to get there, but they will! I make my bed about 98% of the time now. I have some kids who make their bed on their own, and others who still haven't figured this out, but they will.

<u>13 – Choose to feel gratitude</u>

Part of the reason why I avoided housework was because I hated it. It was just going to get messy again. It was boring. What changed for me was when I started to choose to feel grateful for the opportunities I had to be cleaning and serving my family. I do love the feeling of order and cleanliness in my house. I could practice and become better! I looked forward to cleaning up and creating order.

CHAPTER 26
Habits and Self-Discipline

Earlier in this book, I talked about the importance of leading the way. You can certainly lead the way in academics.

Way more important than academics is learning good habits and learning how to GET good habits. That is a skill humans need for the rest of our lives, if we want to move forward on the hero journey. We could just stay home and eat soup and not worry about it, which sounds comfortable, but really isn't since we'd know we weren't growing.

Many of the great philosophers have noted the power of small and simple actions. It is the small habits that create our identity, that create who we really are. It's easy to think that if we do one great action we will become a hero. But it's really the little things that make us great and move us forward.

In the 19th century poem, "Little Things," written by Julia Carney, she highlights this idea:

> Little drops of water,
> Little grains of sand,
> Make the mighty ocean
> And the pleasant land.

It is like that in our lives. The small daily habits we have form our character and who we are. Have you heard some of these quotes from these great minds?

"Our character is basically a composite of our habits. Because they are consistent, often unconscious patterns, they constantly, daily, express our character."

Steven Covey

"We are what we repeatedly do. Excellence,
then, is not an act, but a habit."

Will Durant

"The law of harvest is to reap more than you sow. Sow
an act, and you reap a habit. Sow a habit and you reap
a character. Sow a character and you reap a destiny."

James Allen

Why do I tell you all this? Because if you train your kids to do chores, they can mostly keep the house clean! Best shortcut to cleaning the house ever. If you have all young kids you can't see this yet, but it's so awesome when you can tell the kids to do their chores in the morning, and they do, and your house is clean. If you're only homeschooling for an hour a day, you'll have time for this training! (I put this first!)

However, as I discovered, you can't actually train your kids, if you haven't got the discipline yourself. Kids don't do as you say, they do as you do!

CHAPTER 27
Self-Discipline

As we discipline our children to obey and to have good habits, that is the beginnings of character development. What comes next is helping them learn self-discipline.

Self-discipline is different than discipline. That's when you move on from having someone else tell you what to do. Your mother isn't there anymore to nag you! In order to have self-discipline, one must still have someone to follow. Whom do you follow when you are trying to attain self-discipline? The obvious answer would be to follow yourself if you are to have self-discipline.

But like most true principles of life, the real answer is paradoxical. In order to have the greatest self-discipline, you can't just be following yourself.

Now we can wax philosophical for a few moments. You can't follow yourself because who are you really? What do you really want?

If you can't learn to control yourself, then you will not control what you do, and you cannot become who you are meant to be. As you become who you are meant to be, you find happiness. If you simply seek for happiness, you will never get there.

Most great philosophers and religions agree that to become who you are meant to be, to learn and to grow, you need to serve others. Serving others is what brings happiness. If you can't control yourself through self-discipline, you are actually mostly focused on yourself! You won't be using your time and energy to help others because you'll be using your time and energy to avoid doing your duty by blaming others, being depressed, beating yourself up, and/or complaining about it.

If you want to become more self-disciplined, you need something bigger than you to focus on. If I'm doing something just for myself, my motivation is not nearly so big as if I'm doing it for something bigger than me—such as my family, my friends, my community, a cause, my God.

This is a beautiful paradox: The more I focus on something bigger than me, the more

I see I must become better and focus on myself. As I focus on living in my true self of excellent character by developing self-discipline, the less selfish I become. The less selfish I become, the more people I help around me. The more people I help around me, the happier I am!

As a young mom, I had no idea that the root of most my troubles with my kids was me. I assumed that if my kids were disobedient or acting up, it was because they were acting badly and were bad kids sometimes.

It was a two-fold problem. First, I didn't have the knowledge of how to teach them to obey. Secondly, I didn't have the skill of self-discipline to implement any knowledge I might have.

Fortunately, over the years, I've gained the knowledge, and I've gained the skills needed to do this. I'm certainly not perfect at it, but I'm generally good enough, and I can keep on improving.

This, my friends, is just what you can do too. If messy, disorganized, seriously un-disciplined me can do this, anyone surely can.

I went to bed way too late, rationalizing that it was my only time to to get things done and that I was a night owl. I wouldn't get enough sleep and was a grumpy mom the next day to my kids. I couldn't get them to obey. I would yell and get mad at them, and I'd be mad at myself for being mad at them. I couldn't seem to stay up on the chores and my house was a disaster. My husband didn't really want to be around me (who could blame him? Oh that's right! I could!) and our marriage suffered. I never exercised. I didn't take care of myself. Of course I was supposed to be homeschooling but it was either that full of struggles or trying to pull it together enough to get the house clean and the food on the table. Frozen chicken nuggets or something equally unhealthy, but food. It wasn't all bad, but mostly it was chaotic, a mess and I knew things could be better.

Can you relate to any of that? Did you do what I did? At every new year, I'd set goals and I'd say to myself, "This is the year I'm going to get organized!" Then the next year, I'd pull out last year's goals and say, "Oh shoot. I didn't do that. This is the year I'm going to get organized!"

This went on for years and years so I just gave up on New Year's resolutions. I read hundreds of self-help books. I'd think to myself, "Oh yeah. That's a great idea. I should do that." And then I wouldn't.

Part of the problem was that I thought of myself as a mess. "I am a seriously disorganized person" is what I thought. It was not until I could start seeing myself as a hero on the hero journey, that I could begin to make changes in my life.

The first step was I needed to become aware that I was the problem. You can do that too. This is really empowering because then once you figure this out, you can do something about it! **This is the call to action on the hero journey.**

Most people can't hear this call to action telling them that they have something they need to change. That's because if you have something to change, your brain will take that as evidence that you aren't a good person. As humans, we all want to feel valuable, and we spend a lot of time trying to prove we are enough. But just because you aren't perfect and you do have room for improvement, doesn't mean you aren't good! It simply means you are a human, and when you're willing to recognize that growth opportunity, you step on the path of the hero journey. You will have a refusal about why you shouldn't listen to the call to action. Your brain will try to blame someone else or convince you that you aren't good enough to do this. That's part of the journey, so recognize that, and then choose to keep moving forward.

The next step is to commit to action after deciding that you can do this. Take responsibility for your own actions and stop trying to make everyone else do what you think they should be doing. This is the commitment This is such a trap for moms! If only our kids would just do everything we think they should! But we don't want little robots with their mothers always telling them what to do. Instead, focus on what you in your life to make changes. That's leading the way.

Next you have to change how you do things. If you want your kids to be heroes on the hero journey, then you have to take that journey too. The journey is one of change, and usually the changes are small things, and especially of consistent good habits.

I learned, I read, I took classes, I got mentors, I changed the way I thought about things, I acted, and I am becoming. You can do that too. In this whole process, I learned the principles of change and how to implement them in my own life. What I learned made my life so much better, that I knew I wanted to teach others more about it so they didn't have to struggle as much as I did.

I started teaching these principles to help people like me who couldn't figure out how to create new habits or how to discipline themselves. If you want to educate your kids, to train and guide them, you need to lead the way.

If you want your kids to do things, you put in the work first and learn it yourself first. You wish there was more reading in your home? Read. You don't have to do everything you want them to do. If you see they are avoiding doing something you think they should, look at yourself and do what you're avoiding! Just pick one thing that you've been getting a call to action to do and do it!

As you do this, you'll figure out what motivates you to do what you don't really want to do, but know that you ought to. You'll see how you can help your kids do the same. Plus the good news is that the more focused you are on disciplining yourself, the less hard you are on your kids!

I never ever thought I, of all people, would be writing a book with chapters on how to be self-disciplined. I guess it's true what they say—your mess is your message, meaning those hard things in your life you have overcome are the things you want to help others with. But I can tell you that I now know how to create any new habit in my life. Even the really, really hard ones. The good news is that I am not perfect so I have lots more journeys to go on! I now am in bed most nights by 10:30, which is still amazing to me considering I used to go to bed at 2 am (for 20 years!). I keep a mostly clean house (or can at least get it clean within 20 minutes). I drink water now (I was so dehydrated). I serve homemade healthy food every night for dinner. I've been off sugar for a year. I homeschool my kids consistently. I've implemented obedience and chore training systems. I have a much better marriage. I, the total non-exerciser, ran a half-marathon in just over 2 hours. It hasn't been easy, but I can do it! And so can you!

Why do I tell you all this? It is not to brag, but rather to let you know that you can lead the way no matter where you are, and to give you an example of the beautiful paradox. When I decided that I wanted to lead the way for my kids (for them, not me!), I knew I had to become better and focus on myself. As I have focused on living in my true self of excellent character by developing self-discipline, the less selfish I have become. The less selfish I have become, the less I feel the need to control everyone else around me and the more I can allow and encourage them on their journeys. This allows me to help a lot more people, and the more people I help, the happier I am!

CHAPTER 28

Progress, not Perfection

As you try to train yourself and your kids, look for progress, not perfection! We don't have to be perfect on the journey. If we were perfect there would be no progress. It's how we learn and grow.

We get to learn to clean our house to build our character. We teach our children how to clean the house to help them build character. It's a huge part of homeschool!

Teaching them discipline and routine is key. It's something that has to be done every single day. It's something we don't always want to do, but we can change our attitudes.

It starts with you. For those of you like me, it does not come naturally. When I was a young mom with a couple of small kids, I went to my friend's house (who had more kids than I did). I was so impressed at how clean her house was. I asked her, "How do you keep your house so clean?" I think she was a little surprised at my question, because it came so easily to her. She said, "Oh, I just make sure I wash the dishes and tidy up at night before I go to bed." Yes, something that had seriously never even crossed my mind.

For some of you, being disciplined and routined is easy. But you get frustrated when people throw your system off! I knew a woman who had an amazingly beautiful and immaculate house, but she was so stressed about it! Her kids couldn't even sit on the couch.

If you're not disciplined, your learning opportunity is to learn how not to be frustrated or to give up when there is disorder and to also learn how to choose to do it when you simply don't want to or you feel overwhelmed. You know where overwhelm comes from? It comes from thinking you have to have your vision of perfection accomplished right now. But you don't. There are times and seasons.

If you're disciplined, your learning opportunity is to learn to manage your emotions and learn patience with others who haven't learned it yet. Learn to allow messes in your home. That's how they learn creativity, and cleaning it up when they are done is how they grow and build character.

When your kids take piano lessons, do you expect them to be playing Beethoven after just one week? Of course not! We know that it takes learning the foundations first and then even that takes a lot of practice before you can get to the point where you're making real music and it's automatic.

I know that sometimes I'll be training a kid to be obedient and I expect that child to be quite good at it after not much practice. I'll get frustrated and think, "Why aren't you getting this? You should know this by now, I've already taught you!" But clearly they don't! It helps to remember they just need more practice. Just like in piano, some will pick it up faster than others, and for some it will take way more practice than you'd ever think. But they will get there!

Part of the problem I've had when trying to discipline and train my kids is that *I'm* not disciplined enough to be consistent for as long as it takes. So when they don't get disciplined as quickly as I want them to, I get frustrated with THEM, even though it's really me!

This is not to say I have to be actively training my kids all the time. Usually it really only just takes a few weeks of intentional training and then brush up training (and remembering they are still practicing). Sometimes we have to revisit the intentional training too.

One great tip I got for becoming more disciplined was to decide and act fast. I'd heard that successful people do this, but I didn't really know what that meant until I started paying attention to this in my own life.

If I wanted to become more disciplined/successful in having a clean house, how would that even work? Well, each day I needed to do certain things to keep the house clean. Before learning this tip, I would see the dishes and messy counter in the kitchen and think, "Oh, I should clean that up." Then I'd walk by and think it again. The next time I would think, "Why is the kitchen so messy? It's never clean!" It would spiral down from there, until I was feeling overwhelmed like I had too much to do.

I thought to myself that I could apply this principle of success. Would it work if I just decided I would clean up the kitchen after breakfast each morning and then did it? I decided that I would do that. The first morning was great. I had decided and I did it. The next few mornings were great too. But then "stuff" started coming up. You know how it is. An early morning eye exam. A kid with something he needed help with.

I would not get it done and I would not ever gain a new habit in that area, and then I'd beat myself up for being such a lazy person.

The trick is to keep deciding that you will do it every day no matter what! Decide that you are the kind of person who does this every day because you enjoy a clean house. Then even when things come up, you do it anyway. That's power and that's discipline.

Then, the great thing is that once you've been doing this for a while, you have a habit and you no longer have to make the conscious decision to act. You just do it.

Creating a new habit can take a lot of energy, but once you've got it, it saves you a lot of energy! That's because you no longer have to decide to do it.

Making decisions takes a lot of energy. Why is that? Because making decisions is hard if you think you have to make the right decision all the time. If you make a wrong decision, then you might mess up, and if you mess up, you might not be a valuable human being. You don't even realize you are doing that to yourself. But we avoid making decisions because we don't want to make the wrong choice, and we make a lot of excuses or reasons to avoid deciding. When you avoid making decisions, you get overwhelmed!

Let me give you an example of how this can work in your life. I never could get good at menu planning until I figured this one thing out. Most of the time I would avoid sitting down to plan menus because I knew it would take me forever to decide what was for dinner. I decided to apply the wisdom of deciding fast when choosing meals. I gave myself a time limit of about 20 minutes to decide all the meals for the week. What if I chose a bad meal? Well, then I could learn from that and not choose it again! What if some of the kids didn't like it? They can eat it or not! It was OK to be wrong and make a mistake. This new way of looking at menu planning made this activity totally doable for me so I have been planning my menus regularly for the last few years on a consistent basis.

Maybe menu planning is easy for you. But I bet there is some other area in your life that you are struggling in, and part of that struggle comes from simply avoiding decisions. What is that for you?

Keep on recognizing what you are doing well! You are! You are on this journey, and if you've been stuck, it's ok, you can start moving again. You are a hero and so are your kids.

PART 4
STAY SANE

CHAPTER 29

Sanity

The full title of this of this book is "How to Get Everything Done: Homeschool and Clean the House and Stay Sane". Of course I'm saying stay sane in kind of a joking way. I'm talking about how people use this outside of mental hospitals, when we tend to exaggerate after a stressful, difficult day and say we are losing our sanity!

Sanity really just means you have a healthy state of mind. You are able to think and behave in a normal, functional, and rational manner.

Some synonyms for sanity are: sense, wisdom, prudence, rationality. It also comes from the Latin word "sanitas," which means health.

Basically it means that you are able to choose how you respond to what happens in your life, and that you feel healthy and you feel good about life!

On the hero's journey, when we hit those obstacles, they can cause us to have a lot of different feelings! When you start having too many negative feelings, and you get overwhelmed; you're not feeling too sane. You may feel like you're going crazy and at the same time, you're going nowhere; you're stuck!

That's what we call stuck in the wilderness of your journey. It's not a fun place to be, and it's not where you want to be, because you want to feel slightly sane; to be able to think and behave in a normal, functional manner. Plus you've still got that whole "I have to get everything done" thing hanging over your head.

In this book, we've mostly been talking about a part of your journey: homeschooling and cleaning. But what about when you feel like you're wandering or stuck in the wilderness? That's where "stay sane" comes into play.

As I was pondering this, I came up with three things that help us stay sane—and feel good about life. We feel good about life even if it's not perfect when we are moving forward on our journey. It is these three concepts that help us along our path:

1. Give up control
2. Get control
3. Progress and purpose

Give up control! I can't do that! Don't worry, because in #2, you'll get some too.

CHAPTER 30

Control, Motivation, and Stressed-out Mommas

The first thing I mentioned to stay sane was to give up control. I don't mean abandon all control; don't worry. But what I do mean is that we spend way too much time trying to control things that aren't really ours to control.

As humans we have a need for control. We like to feel in control.

We worry so much about making sure everything around us is under control—our control. There is that part of us that really wants to have the Pinterest-perfect home and kids, ya know what I mean?

Some of the things around us are things that should be under our control. But when it comes to people, our kids and husbands especially, we can't control them. But we still try to anyway. We tell ourselves that we're just helping them by trying to make them do things, but that isn't a truth.

Does your husband do anything that drives you nuts? Or not do things you think he should do? For most of us I'm guessing that's a resounding yes. Mine sure has. To protect the innocent I won't go into detail what those things are, but when he does something annoying or doesn't do things that would help himself or me out, what do I do about that? Well, I get annoyed. Then I start thinking all sorts of negative things about him. Even if I don't say anything, he can tell. I act annoyed, I send off annoyed vibes. While he may or may not figure out why I'm annoyed, the problem is really mine. But in my brain, I'm thinking HE should change. That is my little form of trying to control him. It doesn't work one whit. Have you ever done this? Does it work for you?

We end up causing ourselves so much stress because we say we are worrying about our kids and husband. We feel responsible for fixing them! But ladies! They aren't broken! They aren't perfect either, but they aren't bad! They are amazing human beings, here on this earth on their own hero journeys!

When I try to shame or blame or complain others into doing what I think they should be doing, that is manipulative. I'm using my emotions to manipulate their emotions to get them to act the way I want them to in order to get my approval. It doesn't work. Why do I do that? It's because I can't let go of the idea that I need to control them because I know what is best for them. I do know some things that are best, but is it isn't really responsibility to choose how they act. If I can't let go and let them learn on their own path and timeline, it's often because I'm struggling with traveling that path in my own life. I don't believe that I am good enough to take this journey. I have a belief that if I mess up, I'm a failure. If my kids mess up and I'm supposed to be in charge, then I really must be a failure.

I want my kids (and husband) to learn and grow and do great things. I want them to be successful. You want that for your kids (and husband) too! But how do you get them to do what you think they should? How can you let go and let them go on their journey? How do you motivate the kids? How do you inspire them?

Motivation is getting people to do things you think they should do. Inspiring them is helping them decide to do things they think they should do. We can use both; however, motivation can still be manipulative if we tie our own self-worth to how our children act. We have to take ourselves out of it and love them no matter what choices they make.

CHAPTER 31

Stop Worrying, Start Believing

At some level you already know this, and yet, you still worry. There are two different kinds of worry:

Productive worry – you can change something about how you think or act.

Non-productive worry – you worry about things that aren't yours to change. You beat yourself up and fear you are failing your kids, or your husband will never get it right. The reason you fear this is because you fear deep inside that you're not perfect. That's a problem because if you aren't perfect, you might not be worthy of love. You feel like you have to fix them to prove that you're worthy.

This is some important human psychology here. What human beings crave the most is love and acceptance. People who feel loved and accepted as they are, feel safe to be vulnerable enough to change, to learn and to grow. When children have a good example (not perfect), they know they are loved, and they are surrounded with ideas of greatness. That's inspiring.

If a human doesn't feel loved and accepted, they will choose to act in certain ways to gain love and acceptance. As no human being feels loved and accepted all the time, we all tend to do one or both of the methods I'll explain below. People aren't necessarily one or the other; they may choose different methods at different times with different people.

Think about these methods with respect to yourself and your kids and what methods you and they mostly choose:

PLEASER – One method is the "pleaser" method, where we do what others say in order to get acceptance from others. If we aren't perfect, we can't please everyone, and we will beat ourselves up because we can't measure up. Listen to the words of what you and your kids say to recognize this: Oh, I'm so dumb. I can't do anything right. I'm stupid.

JUSTIFIER – People justify their actions so that they can still feel OK about themselves. We will either do that by rationalizing that we are ok, or we justify our actions by saying others or circumstances are stopping us. What do they say? "You hate me" "She always messes me up!" "I just didn't have time." "Well if he hadn't told me at the last minute."

If someone chooses the pleaser method, they will do what you want them to do either to get you off their back (so it's out of fear), or they will do it to make you love them (which makes them a doormat).

If someone choose the justifier method, then you're going to experience a difficult relationship, or rebellion. You are going to have power struggles.

I'm betting that you can start to recognize all of these. When you first start homeschooling, your child usually wants to please you; you were both excited! Kids who are choosing "pleaser" are usually pretty compliant and do what you say, but they don't really build confidence in themselves because their worth all depends on how you react to them. These seem to be the kids who are "easy" to homeschool.

When things get hard, they feel the inner rebellion, and the justifying begins in them, and the worrying starts in you and you go into this spiral of power struggle and on the road to burnout. Some kids just start out with that inner rebel as the justifier. Kids like that seem hard to homeschool!

So you have either doormat or rebel running our lives, and both of them are based in the same root cause: fear. Fear that you won't be loved and accepted. Fear that you aren't enough.

If someone is worried about you, you will not feel love or acceptance. You'll feel like something is wrong with you. You may feel rebellious, but then you will create stressful relationships.

Clearly this doesn't work.
You need a better way.

Let me give you some more practical examples so you can get what I'm saying here.

I used to never exercise. My husband was worried about me. He didn't ever directly say anything to me, but I got the signals. Did that make me want to change? For some people, they will try to change because someone else worried about them and they feel bad. They try to change out of fear. "Oh, I'm a failure because I don't exercise. But he thinks I should, so I'd better so he will like me." But the changes could never last because they weren't changing for the right reasons. For other people, like me, I just started rationalizing more. I thought, "oh my husband is worried about me. But I'm fine. I don't have to exercise. I run up and down the stairs a lot chasing kids. I'm still fine. Besides he doesn't know how hard it is for me. He's so judgmental. Plus he should support me."

Think about your kids. What if they aren't getting math? We tend to worry about them. Even if you never say anything, they know you are worried. You're worried so they don't have to worry about it; they'll just let you do it. It's easier anyway. Some of your kids will be pleasers and do it anyway, and they'll do it out of fear, or to please you. Other of your kids will feel the inner rebel and you'll have power struggles which will increase your stress and anxiety level and make you feel like you're failing.

What do you do instead?

You have to let go of the idea that you can control any of the people in your life, or any of the events in your life.

Then stop worrying and start believing.

Believe that YOU are enough.

Believe that THEY are enough.

Believe that you are a hero moving forward on your journey and that it's OK if you wander sometimes.

Believe that they are a hero moving forward on their journeys and that it's OK if they wander sometimes.

It doesn't really matter what pictures you hang on your walls and what books you read to your kids, you won't have that safe environment until you learn how to properly use control. You worry as a form of control. You are trying to make them change by worrying about it. You might try to use force, bribes, rewards, etc. But all of those are because you're worried and because you're trying to control them.

CHAPTER 32

More on Worry

Let's go talk a bit more about worry. Worry just means a state of anxiety and uncertainty over actual or potential problems.

I used to think I was pretty chill, that I never really worry. Especially when I would compare myself to my husband, who tends to worry about worst-case scenarios, like when it's windy he can't sleep because the shingles might fly off the roof. But boy, did I ever worry about what everyone else was doing or not doing! Both of us would be non-productively worrying because we couldn't do anything about it, except change the way we thought or acted—and neither of us were.

Everyone has worries. But where does this worry come from? Why do we worry?

Worry is part of our human condition because we need it for survival. We needed worry to kick us into physical preservation. If we didn't worry, we'd just go right up to a wild animal and then it would eat us, or walk across a busy freeway without looking. Worry is there to keep us alive.

Worry is a natural state. It's the path of least resistance. In nature, the natural state is to go back to wild nature, to chaos. But remember! Humans aren't here to just go with the "natural state." We are here to become, and to create order out of chaos. To do that, we must go against the natural state and create something better! That's hard work! Worry is a natural state of humans—and it brings us to chaos. Chaos is simply a signal we need to realign something to bring things back to order. If we have too much worry, it brings us into overwhelm where we don't do anything. Alternatively, we can recognize it and let it move us to action.

The word "worry" comes from an old English word, "wrygan," which actually means "to strangle." In the 16th century the word worry meant "to assault verbally." In the 17th century it meant "to bother, distress or persecute." Now it means "to feel anxious or distressed or troubled or uneasy." When we worry we are strangling ourselves! We are also sending out signals of distress and anxiety.

We have created stories in our childhood that cause stress and worry in our lives. We took those stories from our childhood and brought them into our adult life. We still use these stories subconsciously to protect ourselves and avoid pain. But often, these are false stories we created when we were little. It's important to recognize where some of these beliefs that are no longer serving us are coming from. Better yet, we can create new stories that help us progress and don't keep us stuck in the muck.

When we're on the hero's journey, many of these get amplified when we run into obstacles! But that's why the obstacles are there. It's so we can realize what we are thinking that is stopping us.

Here are some stories we have created in our brains that cause us to worry:

Insecurity ("I live in a threatening world.")

> We want to protect our kids, so maybe we get overprotective, and we worry about them.

Perfectionism ("If I make mistakes, I will be a failure.")

> We need mistakes to grow! If we were perfect, we wouldn't need to grow, but that's what we need to do as humans.

Need for control ("If I lose control, I am in danger.")

> No one wants to feel out of control. When we feel like we are out of control, we worry. But we can't control other people or circumstances; we can only control ourselves and how we react, and of course that's the hardest person to control.

Social comparison ("People will think I'm a loser.")

> If we're bucking social norms (and we do this when we choose to homeschool), we will worry about what people think!

Pessimism ("I never get what I want." "I don't have enough")

> Eeyore syndrome! "It looks like rain." If we think we don't have what we need, we never will.

Low tolerance for stress ("How can I protect myself if I'm all stressed out?")

> If we don't know how to manage our thoughts and emotions, we will get stressed out. When we're stressed, we worry more. We want to help our kids live up to their greatness, but we're not going to do it by worrying about them. Instead, we do this by inspiring them and creating a safe environment in which they can learn and grow.

It's not an environment where we are making sure they learn everything they need to know when they need to know it. We feel like we need to make sure our children are succeeding and doing certain things at certain times. When they don't we feel like a failure and we start worrying more!

Clearly, worry isn't really productive, it doesn't help change things and it doesn't help us keep our sanity. Worry is really a way we are trying to control things in our world.

But we can be grateful for worry because it's a signal we are trying to control what is not ours to control.

How do you stop worrying? How do you let go of those things that are not yours to control?

First you have to recognize what you are doing.

Then it's time to take responsibility for your thoughts. I used to think I took responsibility for my own thoughts, but I wasn't really. I was simply justifying them. Our brains really, really don't like to be wrong. It always looks for evidence that it is right, and we'll get more thoughts to rationalize why we are right. But if what I'm thinking doesn't point towards truth or happy feelings, it's not right. I can take responsibility for my thoughts by choosing the ones that will make me and those around me better. I can take responsibility by choosing the thoughts that are good about the things I can and cannot control.

If I can't control it, then I need to let it go.

If I can, I can choose other ways of looking at it than to keep on worrying. I can let my worry be productive and move me to action.

The best way I've found to stop worrying and controlling is to fill it in with something better. The two best thoughts I can choose are:

> Belief
> Gratitude

If I can choose to believe in the goodness and greatness of people, I can allow them to take their own journey.

If I can choose to find gratitude in ANY situation, I can feel happiness and control of my own life.

To review, what do you do instead?

1. Stop worrying and start believing

   a. Your kids can feel you worry. They create stories in their heads about themselves. You did that too when you were a kid.

   b. I can't control what my kids do. I can only control myself. But I can allow them choices and help them grow and progress with failure and successes.

   c. Use better words and tone of voice. Be encouraging.

   d. Create instead of stunt growth. Creation is progress. Fear is stuck.

2. Offer, don't force

   a. What if they don't want to? They fail. They can learn from that.

   b. If they don't take it, you still love them.

   c. Know the difference between rewards, bribes and consequences and when to use them.

3. Provide examples

   a. Learn about heroes and the hero journey

   b. Find other amazing people to be around

   c. Read great books with examples of heroes

   d. Lead the way with your own example

      i. Get a passion, a hobby! (Then you won't hover.)

      ii. You don't have to do exactly the things you want them to do. You just have to be progressing.

If I choose to believe that my kids are inherently good, and want to grow and progress, I can simply choose to love, uplift and believe in my kids. It's much less stressful.

CHAPTER 33

Be Controlling

In the previous chapters, I talked about how we had to let go the control of those things that aren't ours. But as human beings we don't like the feeling of "out of control." We do need some control in our lives. Instead of trying to control everyone else, focus on controlling the things that you are responsible for.

Which are:

1. How you think
2. How you act
3. How you react to other people and circumstances in your life.

Basically, the only thing you really can control is you.

I have to learn to control myself? It's so much easier to worry about everyone else!

That means that you learn self-discipline and self-care.

We all know what self-discipline is, right? It's doing what you said you would. It's having integrity with yourself. If you said you were going to exercise three times this week, you do it. This is all about forming good habits and character in yourself—exactly what you want for your kids, right?

You lead the way!

When I first began homeschooling, I didn't think I was organized enough to do it. But let's face it. I really just didn't have any self-discipline to create habits and routines to keep things organized and structured. I just thought, "Oh, I'm not naturally organized. I can't do that."

Some people are "born organized." I was not one of those people. But I found out that it was just a skill like any other—that comes easier to some people, but all people can learn it. It is just a matter of disciplining yourself to do what needs to be done, and to create good habits.

CHAPTER 34

Self-Care and Sanity

You knew this chapter was coming. How can you have a book on staying sane and not talk about self-care?

Self-care is a subset of self-discipline because it takes discipline to care for yourself. Often the first thing you think of when you think of self-care is something like taking time to go get nails done, sometimes called "me time." While "me time" is great, this isn't really what is meant by self-care.

Quite frankly, homeschool moms are terrible at self-care. We feel so anxious trying to fit it all in, but we can't, so the first one to go is ourselves. We become mother-martyrs. We get angry or depressed. No fun.

I've pondered on this a lot because I too have been terrible at it. I didn't want to be selfish; I wanted to give my all to my family. But if I have nothing to give from, I can't do that.

You've probably all heard the "fill your cup" or the "put your oxygen mask on first" analogies. You can't give from an empty cup, nor can you help others if you can't breathe. But I never knew how to do that. How do I fill the cup? How do I put my oxygen mask on first without being selfish?

I love reading stories of of ancient people, because typically if they have lasted this long, there is are principles to learn from them. One story that comes to mind here is the story of King Solomon in the Old Testament. He follows his father, King David, as the king of Israel. He was honored by his people. He was very wise and extremely wealthy, and was a good king to his people. He had it all!

As he grows more famous and wealthy, he lives a life of massive self-indulgence and worldly treasures. He begins to lose his focus, direction and purpose. At the end of his life, he sums it all up as "All is vanity."

In other words, he was living a selfish life, where it was all about him, and he regretted it.

As humans we have an interesting conflict. Our bodies really just want to be comfortable and feel good. We like sitting on the coach and vegging, rather than get up and do what we think we should. We enjoy junk food more than eating healthy foods. It's the "natural state" of our bodies; it's chaos.

But inside of us, we have a spark of light, a goodness that is in all of us that wants more, and that's where we have the conflict. We feel guilty for not doing what we think we should. It is a battle between our body and our inner desires.

Our brain is kind of like the go-between in this conflict. Your brain mostly came set with a scarcity mentality. It's looking out for you and it wants to keep your body alive. When you feel uncomfortable, it will try to keep you comfortable in order to keep you alive. It wants to be right, so whatever you are thinking about, it will look for proof that your thoughts are true. If you are thinking a refusal about why you can't act on a call to action, your brain will show you why you can't. For example, you might think, "I don't have any money, so I can't sign up for this class." Unless you are paying attention, you will let this refusal stop you from moving forward on what you wanted to do. You may also think that is very reasonable and rational.

Your brain is just a tool, though. You can train it to think differently, and in fact, I believe that's really a big purpose of our lives. We can train our brains to think with an abundance mentality. If you don't act on a call to action because you don't have any money, you are letting the natural state of things rule you. Instead, you could say to yourself, "I really want to take this class. How can I get the money I need?"

Your brain is amazing! It loves trying to solve problems, so when you ask good questions, it will give you good answers! If you ask yourself that question, you will figure out a way. Then you can act on your call to action!

That wasn't really a tangent. It really is the core of self-care. What does self-care really mean? Self-care is learning to control yourself and regularly doing the things that add power and energy to your life. So it means that you have to put in the effort to do that for yourself instead of trying to control everyone else.

It means choosing to believe you are good and that you a hero on the hero's journey. Because you are a hero, you take time to care for your body by exercising, eating well, drinking water, and getting the sleep your body needs (well, insofar as possible for a mom; you can at least go to bed earlier!). You need to find your purpose and to take the time to connect to your power source. You take time to care for your mental health by training your brain to get out of this beat-up self (or rationalizing) mode and filling your brain with good thoughts to drown out the negative ones, and you keep doing it. You take time to care for your spiritual health, your financial health, and so on, all because you decided you were worth it.

When I see moms who are completely overwhelmed, depressed, angry, etc., it's usually because they aren't taking time to care for themselves. You feel like you don't have the time, but usually it's just because you haven't disciplined yourself to do it!

You're not ignoring your kids, you're empowering your kids. When you choose to take time every day to learn to discipline yourself and take care of you, it empowers them to do the same, because of course that's what you want for them too.

In the book, *Twelve Rules for Life* by Jordan Peterson, Rule #2 is "Treat yourself like someone you are responsible for helping." He talks about a study where they found that people were better at filling and properly administering prescription medication to their pets than they are to themselves!

You are worth taking care of!

If you are going to homeschool, clean the house, and stay sane, you must learn to get the habits to take care of yourself, or you will burn out, or worse.

I do remember feeling completely overwhelmed. I mean, I was keeping the kids alive, but life was chaotic. I was trying to do everything for everyone else. I wasn't filling my cup at all. I also had to learn that filling my cup wasn't about self-indulgence, but self-care of those things that added energy to my life. I wasn't exercising, getting enough sleep, reading my scriptures, praying, eating healthy or any of that. I wasn't creating order in my house or setting boundaries. I was eating ice cream at night a lot though!

What is self-indulgence? I have pondered this because I think there is a fine line between self-indulgence and self-care. Self-indulgence is basically defined as the "excessive gratification of one's own appetites, desires, or whims." You do what you want to do because it feels good to your physical body. Your physical body really does just want to feel comfortable and look good to others. This is not to say that this is wrong. But it's that natural inclination back to chaos that we are trying overcome by creating more good in our lives. The problem comes when this is our go-to, when it becomes excessive and we aren't caring for ourselves because we are indulging ourselves instead. Eating ice cream is self-indulgence because it feels good to my physical body (at least while I'm eating it). It doesn't mean I can't ever do it, though.

It just shouldn't be the replacement for self-care.

Self-care, then, is what feels good to our inner conscience. It's what adds more energy and power to our lives. It's what helps us create more good in our lives. Self-care includes taking care of our physical bodies instead of just doing what "feels good." It also includes taking care of our mental and spiritual health as well, by learning how to manage our thoughts, talk nicely to ourselves, and how to listen to our inner conscience that leads us to good.

Our physical state is often in conflict with our inner values! That's why too much self indulgence feels lousy and doesn't really help us feel better. Self-care is what gets us back into alignment with our core goodness.

Sometimes, I still feel overwhelmed. That's when I know I need to step up my self-care efforts so I can deal with it better. But at the same time, I also need to recognize that I can't do it all and some things just need to be taken off the plate, and I need a break.

When I first heard this concept of self-care, I mostly dismissed the idea because it sounded so selfish. As I could see it as something that could add more power to my life, I knew I needed it in my life.

But I still heard the voices that told me I didn't have time for this. It sounded so overwhelming to add another thing! I felt guilty and beat myself up for not doing it. I would hear about people who would get up at 5 am and do a "Power Hour" in the morning.

How would I do that when the baby was keeping me up at night, I was so tired and I was barely hanging on by the skin of my teeth?

I avoided doing things for self-care for myself for a long, long time. I mean, I brushed my teeth and got dressed most of the time. But I didn't do those things that brought more power to my life—like exercising, spending time with God, writing in my journal, going to bed and getting enough sleep and so on. I didn't think I had time for it. But that was really just an excuse because I just didn't have the discipline to do it for myself. I didn't get the discipline because deep down, I really didn't think I was worth it. I would run myself ragged trying to control everyone else, in an effort to prove that I was good.

I decided I really wanted to act on this call to action to bring more power to my life. I didn't know how to do it, so for a long time, I didn't do anything. Finally, I decided to ask. What do I do to bring more power to my life? The answer that came to me was "Just start with something small. Just do one minute a day." I could do that! But because I had a long list of improvements I needed to make, I didn't know which to start with! I asked again. I knew that I just needed to read my scriptures to connect myself to my power source for one minute a day.

That was something I could do. Even though my brain said, "Oh, one minute isn't enough. You have to do more." I wasn't going to do more since I was doing none. I had to tell myself that it was OK to just start with one minute a day! So I did. I wasn't consistent at first, but after awhile, it got easier. I got better at it. I was able to increase my time. I started adding in other good habits. I felt happier and less stressed out and grumpy.

You can do this too. Start where you are! What is your call to action? Why can't you do it? Recognize the refusals, then ask how you can!

I really don't know if I could have done this all without being connected to my power source, which is God. What is your power source? Figure it out, and then listen to how you need to connect to your power source. Because when you're on the hero journey path of motherhood and homeschooling, you can't do it all on your own.

I think God gave us way more to do than we could ever possibly do on our own, simply so we would turn to him. As women we are so capable, but we also are sometimes too independent, and we don't learn to be humble enough to allow him to help us.

When it comes to homeschooling, I can use all these different techniques and get my kids to do the schoolwork I want them to do. But I'm not in the business of simply making sure I check off all the skills for each of my kids and get trained kids who do what they are supposed to. If I was doing that, it'd be way easier just to send them back to school! But I want kids who not only gain skills and training, but who also know who they are, have great character, and who transform as they go forward on their hero's journeys to become the person they are meant to become.

Rather than putting my energy into constantly trying to get the kids to do what they're supposed to, I'd much rather put energy into creating: creating the person I want to become, creating a space for my kids to live up to their potential, creating good in this world instead of more fear.

This all goes back to the character training I talked about earlier. If you want your kids to have good character, you've got to get disciplined yourself first.

I know. You don't have time to take care of yourself, you're too busy taking care of everyone else and the house and homeschooling them! I get it. I bought into that lie too.

Caring for you takes intention, focus and consistency, yes, but it doesn't have to take a lot of time.

Now, as a mom, you do have a lot of things on your plate! If you have babies and toddlers, they do take a lot of time! But you're going to struggle mightily if you don't figure out some way to get some of that self-care. You may have to ask your husband and have him help you out; he likely has no idea that it is a struggle for you. You really cannot do this all by yourself. You have so many good things you want to do, so many things you think you should do, but you literally cannot. Don't beat yourself up for not having everything exactly how you wanted it to be. I wish I had figured this out sooner, but I did eventually get it.

There is a time and a season to go beyond and do more than just the basic maintenance of your home. There are times when you can't even do that, such as when you have a new baby, deal with health challenges, move, or suffer a death in the family. Give yourself permission to be OK with just "getting by" during those times, and ask for and receive help.

From one homeschool mom to another, please stop trying to do everything yourself. I know that most of you are, because it's what we do! You don't have to be a do-it-yourselfer. Just because you can, doesn't mean you always should. When you do that to yourself, you turn into a mother-martyr. Mother-martyrs are on the fast road to burnout.

Sometimes it's so worth it to spend a little extra money on things to help you out. Many of you probably think there is no extra money in the budget, yet you'll spend money on classes for your kids. But you'd never think of hiring someone to come help clean the house twice a month (which is much less expensive than you might think!). You'd probably have a hard time spending money on a course for yourself to learn so you get through your struggles faster, but you'd find a way to hire a tutor if your child was having a tough time with math.

How do I know this? Because it's exactly what I did for many years. All my energy and resources went to my kids and family. I didn't get much of it. I had to decide that I was worth investing in, and that I didn't need to do it all myself.

I also had a realization that I was stuck in scarcity thinking. By that I mean that I never had enough—time, money, energy, support, etc. I was constantly thinking about why I *couldn't* do things rather than asking "what if?" When you shift from thinking of all the reasons you can't to 'what if you could,' it's pretty amazing what can happen. You start noticing opportunities, and if you don't talk yourself out of them, they are there to help you! You are not alone, and you don't have to keep slogging through, doing everything yourself.

Once I decided to open my eyes and see all the abundance of opportunities around me, and stop thinking of the reasons I couldn't have things, I started seeing things in a whole different way!

There was one month in my life that I had a huge project going on, not to mention the daily care for the house and my family. I decided I really wanted to have someone help me prep meals during that especially busy time of life. I had no idea if that was even a thing, or if I could even afford it, but I wanted to be open to that possibility.

About a week after I decided this, I was browsing some online classifieds because I wanted to find an ad that I'd seen earlier for some farm-fresh eggs. While I was searching, I came across an ad that said, "2 Weeks Free of Meal Prep in Your Home." Interesting! I clicked on it to learn more. A lady in my area was testing out a new business idea and really did want to do meal prep for free. As I read through this ad, I started thinking, "Oh, that's too weird. I can't have a stranger come in my house. And I'm so disorganized. I could never do this."

I nearly clicked away from the ad when I heard a voice in my brain say, "This is for you!"

Wow. That was for me. I contacted the lady and told her I was interested. She told me that hardly anyone had contacted her so she was thrilled that I wanted to test out her services.

She was amazing, and we became good friends, and I got free meal prep for two weeks. Then of course because I liked it so much and her prices were not expensive at all, I found a way to hire her to keep on coming back! Truthfully, it saved me a lot of money by having good healthy food prepared instead of buying convenience foods! I never did find the egg-guy, but that wasn't really what I needed then.

This isn't to say that the only way you're going to get everything done is to find someone else to cook or clean for you. But I tell this story because some of us are so darn stubbornly set on that mindset that we need to do it all ourselves, and that we have to do it all ourselves because of lack of money or support or whatever. Sure, I get it. I've been there, done it all myself. But I've also learned that resources aren't usually nearly as limited as we think, and you don't have to run yourself ragged trying to do it all.

You are worth investing in. You don't have to do it all yourself, and it makes you a much happier, saner mom!

CHAPTER 35

Practice Makes Progress

I know I make this all sound so simple. But it is incredibly difficult to change your mindset. If it were easy, we would've changed by now! You've been thinking this way for so long that you probably don't even know it! Most of us have no clue that what we are thinking is stopping us and keeping us in these situations where we just struggle.

I had no idea that it was mostly me that was stopping me for a very very long time. But once I got clued into that, it sure changed my life! This may sound pretty simple and it is, but sometimes you just can't see this for yourself, and that's where a mentor comes in handy. Mentors don't tell you what to do, but they help you see what you can't see in your own life.

Here are a few pointers to start changing your life by changing how you look at it:

First, you've got to be aware of the issue, and then notice what you are thinking that is stopping you. What are you thinking that is keeping you wandering around in the wilderness? You are a hero on the hero journey, but you aren't meant to stay there forever; you're meant to do great things!

Next, choose a new way of thinking. Flip it around to make your thinking more in alignment with the hero that you really are. Heroes don't stay in a complaining or blaming state, nor do they beat themselves up for mistakes, because if they do, they get stuck! Instead, look for something to be grateful for in every situation, whether you think it's good or bad.

Last, keep on practicing! Practice, practice, practice! I spent a lot of time in a concerted effort to flip my thoughts to gratitude. I had to be very intentional about this. I'm certainly not perfect at this, and I do still catch myself complaining or blaming, but I've gotten way better at it. It was a thrilling day when I recognized that my brain was starting to do this automatically!

I had driven to Costco on a beautiful warm day and I was chatting on the phone (which is legal in my state, and I also have HandsFreeLink, so don't worry). Of course because I was talking on the phone, I wasn't totally paying attention to where I parked the car. I walked into the store, still chatting on the phone.

I did my shopping, loading my cart up very, very full because that is what you do when you have seven kids. I checked out, was impressed that the checker actually got it all back into the cart, and went to go show my receipt to the lady at the door. That was when I realized I had no clue where I had parked my car!

My first thought was, "You are so dumb. You should've paid attention to where you parked the car!"

But then, my thoughts automatically went to gratitude. I thought, "But hey! You're going to get a lot of extra steps on your step tracker and you needed more today!"

Then I laughed at myself because this gratitude was so silly, and then I felt grateful that I could see the bright side automatically. After all my practice, it was finally paying off because I didn't have to make any extra effort to think that way in this situation.

Practice is what it's all about. Allow yourself to practice, and allow it of your kids too. It's like learning to play that Rachmaninoff piece. But I promise it gets easier as you practice.

Not long ago, I was riding in the car while my 15-year-old daughter was learning to drive. It is always a very interesting experience to teach a kid to drive a car. If you've ever taught a kid to drive a car you'll able to relate really well, but if you haven't yet, you can think of when you learned. I want her to learn how to drive a car, so took her to the DMV and she got her permit. I gave her some basics and I let her take our car out for driving while I gave her guidance from the front passenger side.

She's pulling out from the driveway and of course I know we're in trouble because she's jerky and she forgot which one was the gas pedal and which one was the brake. I'm sitting there trying not to completely panic as she's about to run into the garage. Admittedly, I have to react quickly and say "STOP! Other pedal!" (ok, yell, "STOP! Other pedal!")

Teaching a teenager to drive is not for the faint of heart. It is definitely a job for a hero-mama! This is because I have pretty much no control over the car. I have to trust her even though I don't totally, but I do know that she can learn this. How do I know? Look at all the other people on the road that have learned this. The only thing I can control is me, and how I react to her. I can get on her and criticize her and I can freak out. Or I can remain calm and encourage her.

Yes, I may have freaked out a few times like when she made that really wide right-hand turn in to the left lane and nearly hit the car that was pulling up in that lane. But I did apologize, and then I went back to encouraging her. I tell her, "That's ok, you're learning, you didn't hit the car, no harm done—but I doubt you're going to do that again! You just need a little more practice, and you'll get it!"

Compare this to how you homeschool. It's actually pretty similar. You can't make your kids learn, you have to let them take the wheel and trust that they will learn. You can facilitate their education by providing the tools they need, the knowledge and guidance they need. You can turn it into a power struggle if you like, or you can let them practice when they are ready and willing to do it! You can try to control how they do things, and how fast they learn it, but that's going right into a power struggle. You can control how you react, and you learn that by practicing, doing it over and over again.

Practice! Look for progress, not perfection. But sometimes you may not even think there is any progress! And that's OK too. It just means they hit a wall; they are struggling. Help them see how to get out of that if they let you, but you can't do it for them. Just like I couldn't make my daughter drive (or even drive well), but I could give her the knowledge and then offer her the opportunity to get the practice she needs, and keep on encouraging her all along the way.

CHAPTER 36
Progress and Purpose

You feel like you're going crazy when you feel overwhelmed. Ah! It's too much! You feel like you're going crazy when you feel depressed. Both of these are situations where you feel like you're wandering around in the wilderness. You feel stuck, and everything starts piling on top of you.

So, the antidote to feeling stuck is to have some purpose. Where are you going? What do you want? What goals are you actively working towards?

Now that doesn't mean that you won't wander. But you'll wander for sure if you don't know what you want. .

Being busy without a bigger purpose makes you feel crazy. Having purpose could mean that you are still busy, or not. The difference is you having purpose.

It seems completely counterintuitive and probably totally overwhelming to think about having to have goals and purpose on top of everything else! But it's what brings peace and order to your life because it gives you something to move towards. You don't feel like you're stuck or wandering.

Your purpose or goals don't even have to be big. They just need to give you a direction. They don't even have to be perfectly right! We just need progress in our lives.

Picture this: When your life is in chaos and you feel stuck and like you're going crazy, it's kind of like all the different elements in your life are puzzle pieces, from different puzzles. You and probably everyone around you is grabbing them and throwing them everywhere, and you're trying to grab them and keep them all but you don't even know if you really need them. But when you begin to decide what you want to create in your life, all of a sudden it's like you have the picture of what puzzle you are making. You realize that it wasn't really as complicated as you were making it after all. When you start working towards smaller goals to create that life, you start to gather the puzzle pieces you need. Then when you start making good habits, it's like you got a bottle of puzzle glue, and those pieces aren't going anywhere!

When you accomplish a goal, it feels good. Feeling good is a great way to stay sane. As you focus on trying to change your world, it starts to change the world around you. When you focus on changing everyone and everything around you, it only leads to frustration, overwhelm, and other things you don't want. Added bonus: you don't have time to control what everyone else is doing because you're too busy controlling you!

Remember, we're looking for progress, not perfection.

Our children are on the hero journey path. They have greatness within. They are on this journey. As you believe they will learn from their failures and keep progressing, they do! But you must lead the way so you can know how it works!

What if you really don't know what you want? About seven years ago, I attended a class where we were all asked to choose something that we really wanted. As a mom of many kids I wasn't really used to this. I had a difficult time thinking of something that I really wanted!

It was September and we had been super busy all summer with vacations and running around. School and all our extracurricular activities had just gotten back into full swing. I wasn't thinking about what I wanted at all; I was just trying to adjust to fall life! But I did know that I'd been so busy I hadn't gotten to buy any fresh peaches. It was the season after all, and that is one thing that I really, really love. Peaches purchased from the grocery store are basically disgusting when compared to a fresh-picked peach. So delicious and yummy!

I decided that was what I wanted! I had no idea how or where I was going to get them. I just decided. Two days later, a friend gifted me with a box of fresh, juicy peaches. Pure heaven!

I learned a valuable lesson from this experience. I realized that it really was OK to want things and that I didn't even have to know how I would get it. I am not selfish just because I have desires for good things!

Of course I don't get everything I want that easily! Other things are much bigger. I just have to decide what I want and not worry about whether it is the right thing or not. As I go after what I want, I will figure it out.

I never knew I wanted to write a book. I just knew I wanted to help other moms who struggled with balancing it all. I got the idea to write a book. So I decided that was what I wanted. If you're reading this, you will see that my purpose was fulfilled, and I got what I wanted.

When I say to choose a purpose, to decide what you want, I obviously don't mean this in a super self-centered way. I trust you to choose something good, because I know you are good inside!

Now one thing to notice is that most people know what they don't want, rather than what they do want. It doesn't work that way, because when you focus on what you don't want, you just get more of that. You need to choose what you do want instead!

I knew I didn't want a messy house or grumpy, complaining kids. You probably don't either. Knowing what you don't want is a start, but you need to figure out what you do want. It wasn't until I could decide that I wanted an organized, clean house with happy, grateful kids that I could focus on that and move towards that purpose!

CHAPTER 37

The Truth About Getting Everything Done

I hope you all know that you can't actually get *everything* done. But you can definitely get all the really important things done. At least mostly.

As I study topics, I love to look for patterns and truths. So here are some that I've been writing down and thinking about with regards to getting things done.

1. Often, getting things done takes a lot longer than you think it should. That's because most of us are really bad at estimating the length of time things take.

2. Getting things done often takes less time than you thought it would. In these cases, you should celebrate the ease in which we got it done, and the gift of time you were given by getting it done faster!

3. Getting things done always takes longer when you have other people involved or around. Which is OK because people are really the point of life.

4. Getting things done like training your kids generally takes much, much, much longer than you think it should. "Shouldn't they know this by know?" we think. But if they don't, then I guess they shouldn't, and we get to learn more patience.

5. At least half of the things you get done (if not more) will not stay done. You will have to to get them done again. That's because we humans need a lot of practice in choosing to be happy no matter what.

6. For most things in life, the things you need to get done don't need to be done perfectly. They just need to be done enough.

7. Many of the things you think you need to get done, you really don't. Some of those things you don't even want to do. So don't do them.

8. Getting things done feels good. Not getting all the things on your list done

doesn't feel good. But your self-worth doesn't depend on what you do or don't get done.

9. You can't manage "time," you can only manage yourself and how you focus and what you do. You are your biggest roadblock to getting things done!

10. You avoid doing things because you don't really want to do them, but often that takes more energy than just doing it!

11. When you think you have more to do than you can do, you feel overwhelmed. When you feel overwhelmed, you avoid doing anything because it seems like it won't help to do such a small amount. The way to get out of overwhelm is to write down everything you think you need to do, pick what is most important to do now and just do it. If all you can do is one thing each day, celebrate that. Then repeat and keep on going.

12. You tend to underestimate how much you have gotten done during a day. Look for what you did do, rather than stew over what you didn't!

CHAPTER 38

You Are a Super Mom

I hope that by now, you realize that you are a hero on the hero journey. You don't have to do it all, nor do you have to do it perfectly. But you do have to keep on going, and lead the way for your kids.

As you recognize yourself in the pattern of the hero journey, your life will become more predictable. As you choose to believe that you are good and you have that greatness inside, your life will become that much more amazing, and you'll see it in your kids too.

As you go, you will learn to trust that you do have the answers and the resources you need, and that you can get them. Your answers and resources will be different than the ones I need, or your kids need, but they are there.

As you keep on going, continuing to learn, and practice, and you're just going to get better and better at this! You really are a super mom!

The hero journey is simple. Not easy, but simple. It's a hard path, but it's so purposeful and fulfilling. It's where you want to go, and it's where I want to help take you.

My purpose is to help moms get on this path to more purpose in their lives, to help them see what they cannot, and to encourage them to keep on going. I would love to hear from you and how I can help you!

You can find me at: https://www.buildingheroesacademy.com, and you can also come join our "Building Heroes" Facebook group at https://www.facebook.com/groups/wearebuildingheroes as a great community to get encouragement and support!

WHERE TO FIND GOOD BOOKS

These are sources I trust to give me direction in choosing good books; however I don't always agree with every single book choice on these lists. It's OK to stop reading a book if you don't like it or it makes you feel uncomfortable!

WEBSITES WITH LISTS OF BOOKS

1000 Good Books List

For fun reading, I choose to go down a recommended level, for more intense reading or read alouds, choose from the suggested level. Found on the "Classical Christian Education Support Loop website: https://www.classical-homeschooling.org/celoop/1000.html

Building Heroes Academy

This is the family-style, principle-based curriculum I wrote, so busy moms could homeschool in an hour a day! I include a read aloud for each month, along with discussion questions that help you connect the stories to your own lives and the principles you're studying. Official website is here: https://www.buildingheroesacademy.com, and you can also watch my webinar about the curriculum at https://www.3homeschoolsecrets.com.

The TJED Classics List

This list is compiled by the DeMilles, who run the Thomas Jefferson Education website. They are the first ones who helped me see some of these ideas I've put in this book. While I've enjoyed most of the books I've read from this list, I haven't liked them all, but that doesn't mean I didn't learn from them. There is a great description of what a "classic" book is, and in my opinion, classics are perfect for reading for ideas of greatness and the hero journey. https://www.tjed.org/resources/classics/.

BOOKS WITH LISTS OF BOOKS

Hunt, Gladys M. *Honey for a Child's Heart: the Imaginative Use of Books in Family Life*. Zondervan Books, 2002.

Mackenzie, Sarah. *Read-Aloud Family: Making Meaningful and Lasting Connections with Your Kids.* Zondervan, 2018.

Trelease, Jim. *The Read-Aloud Handbook.* Penguin Books, 2013.

BIBLIOGRAPHY

Allen, David. *Getting Things Done*. Little Brown, 2019.

Andreola, Karen. *A Charlotte Mason Companion: Personal Reflections on the Gentle Art of Learning*. Charlotte Mason Research & Supply, 1998.

Bauer, Susan Wise, and Jessie Wise. *The Well-Trained Mind: a Guide to Classical Education at Home*. W.W. Norton & Company, 2016.

Campbell, Joseph, and Bill D. Moyers. *The Power of Myth*. Library of Congress, NLS/BPH, 1989.

Christensen, Molly. "Motivation Secrets." *Building Heroes Academy*, 2018, ebook.

Deresiewicz, William. *A Jane Austen Education: How Six Novels Taught Me about Love, Friendship, and the Things That Really Matter*. Penguin Books, 2012.

DeMille, Oliver Van. *A Thomas Jefferson Education: Teaching a Generation of Leaders for the Twenty-First Century*. Thomas Jefferson Education, 2017.

"Dictionary by Merriam-Webster: America's Most-Trusted Online Dictionary." Merriam-Webster, *Merriam-Webster*, www.merriam-webster.com/.

Dunckley, Victoria L. *Reset Your Child's Brain: a Four-Week Plan to End Meltdowns, Raise Grades, and Boost Social Skills by Reversing the Effects of Electronic Screen-Time*. New World Library, 2015.

Juster, Norton, and Jules Feiffer. *The Phantom Tollbooth*. HarperCollins Children's Books, 2008.

Morley, Thomas F. *Once Upon a Brain (Homeschool Edition)*. Sagebrush Innovations, 2009.

"Online Etymology Dictionary | Origin, History and Meaning of English Words." *Online Etymology Dictionary | Origin, History and Meaning of English Words*, www.etymonline.com/.

"Perfectionism." *Psychology Today*, Sussex Publishers, www.psychologytoday.com/us/basics/perfectionism.

Peterson, Jordan B. *12 Rules for Life: an Antidote to Chaos*. Penguin Books, 2019.

Tolkien, J. R. R. *The Hobbit*. HarperCollins, 2008.